How to Care
FOR THE
Whole World
Still Take AND Care
OF
Yourself

A Woman's Complete Guide to Setting Priorities

How to Care for the Whole World and Still Take Care of Yourself

Peg Rankin

Foreword by Patsy Clairmont

BROADMAN
& HOLMAN
PUBLISHERS

Nashville, Tennessee

4253-70
0-8054-5370-9

Dewey Decimal Classification: 248.843
Subject Heading: WOMEN//WIVES//MOTHERS
Library of Congress Card Catalog Number: 94-2431

Unless otherwise noted, all Scripture quotations are from the Holy
Bible, *New International Version*, copyright 1973, 1978, 1984 by
International Bible Society.
Scriptures marked (NASB) are from the *New American Standard Bible*,
© The Lockman Foundation, 1960, 1962, 1963, 1968, 1971, 1973,
1975, 1977, used by permission; (TLB) from *The Living Bible*, copyright
© Tyndale House Publishers, Wheaton, Ill., 1971, used by permission;
and (KJV) from the *King James Version*.

Library of Congress Cataloging-in-Pulication Data
Rankin, Peg.
    How to care for the whole world
    and still take care of yourself / Peg Rankin.
       p. cm.
    ISBN 0-8054-5370-9
    1. Women—Religious life. 2. Christian life—Baptist authors.
    3. Rankin, Peg. I.Title.
BV4527.R36 1994
248.8'43—dc20

                                         94-2431
                                          CIP

This book is lovingly dedicated to my special daughters-in-law—Laurie, Kari-Joy, and Kyra—who are in the midst of what can be "fracturing years." May you find focus and freedom in the pages that follow.

Contents

Foreword

"Start your engines!"

We live in an overwrought world that urges us to accelerate our already overloaded lifestyles. We have lined up as though we are in the Indy 500. Like slick race cars, we are stripped of content, ready to speed off at the drop of the flag. Around the track of life we fly. At the prompting of sideline voices, we increase our breakneck speed. More times than we care to admit we spin out emotionally and cause collisions with fellow racers. We sputter and run low on fuel when we've spent our time driving around and around in circles, which is what whirlwind days feel like.

What a relief when we see through the clouds of dust someone flagging us to take a pit stop. That someone is Peg Rankin. In *How to Care for the Whole World and Still Take Care of Yourself*, she encourages us to stop, look, and listen—stop our road-weary engines, look at our spinning tires, and listen to the one voice that matters.

Peg helps us to distinguish God's voice amidst the roar of all our flighty efforts as well as the shouting demands from those in our grandstand. Once we get an ear for His voice, we will move into a saner lane of existence. Then we can calmly move on at a reasonable pace without crashing into others—and we will make measurable progress. Eventually we will finish the race and move into the winner's circle. Peg is a power-packed woman who drives home truth because she's read the Manual thoroughly and knows the Maker personally.

Have you blown a gasket? Need new spark plugs? Tires a little threadbare? Or maybe you need a complete overhaul? Then pull into the pages of this book. Peg will hoist you up so you can hear His voice calling you to a place and a pace of peace.

—Patsy Clairmont, Author of *Normal Is Just a Setting on Your Dryer* and *Under His Wings*

Preface

On my desk lay a list of proposed book topics. "Do any of these spark your interest?" the publisher asked.

One did: "The Fractured Christian Woman." It virtually leaped off the page.

"But I don't have time to write a book," I argued, trying to silence a cranial computer that was already processing data. "My speaking schedule is too demanding."

I was successful, however, in suppressing the creative urge only so long. One day what was churning in my head started to work its way into my heart.

As I sat down at my desk, I took a personal inventory. I knew I loved the Lord and had dedicated my life to serving Him. I also knew I treasured the church and was grateful for the encouragement it had given me over the past thirty-some years. In addition, I revered God's Word, the all-sufficient power-house of truth. So far so good.

But serving God can become equated with loving Him. I knew that. And the physical organization of the church can be confused with the living organism comprised of human souls. I also knew that. Even the message of the Bible can be misinterpreted as it is taught. Oh, how the Bible teacher in me winced as I was reminded of these dangers.

As I picked up my pencil, I was tense. Then I remembered all the women who, over the years, had shared their pain. Some were career women juggling responsibilities at work, at home, and at church. Others were stay-at-home moms who were inundated with requests to help because they didn't "work." Still others were retired but amazingly busy.

Some of these women were single; others were married. Some were older; others, younger. Most were serious about their faith. And almost all were highly motivated to perform. But one characteristic described every one: they were driven. And, as a result, they were being fractured.

As I thought about these women and the pressures they were

under, their pain came out in the form of voices—voices they were hearing in the world in which they moved. As I examined each message, I realized the truth it represented—awesome truth, tremendous truth. No wonder these voices were trusted!

But then an enlightening thing happened. I discovered the error these messages contained—error so subtle it was hard to pin down, but error devastating enough to keep the Christian woman from becoming all God wants her to be.

I wanted to help these women. But I realized I couldn't help them generally. I would have to be specific. So I chose Laurie, a vibrant thirty-five-year-old mother of three, and decided to write about her. She loves the Lord and wants her life to count. Therefore, she is involved up to her ears in church work. I figured the rest of us could learn a lot from her struggles.

I began my study by enumerating the pressure-messages driving this young woman. I decided to entitle my list:

THE FRACTURED CHRISTIAN WOMAN
(and how to stay that way)

1. Take on more than you can handle. You can never do enough for God.
2. Try to be all things to all people. That's how you show God's love.
3. Strive for greater outreach. One-on-one is fine for starters, but your aim should be the multitudes.
4. Compare your ministry to other people's. If it doesn't measure up, make changes.
5. Gauge the effectiveness of your service by concrete evidence. If you don't see results, there probably aren't any.
6. Set goals and push yourself to achieve them. You want to hear "well done" on Judgment Day.
7. Rarely take time off. There's too much work to be done. You're expected to burn out for God.
8. Tend to your own needs only after you have met everybody else's. Remember how JOY is spelled: Jesus, Others, *then* You.
9. Keep on pouring out, even when there's little left to give. The Christian life is not for quitters.
10. Be willing to sacrifice everything for your ministry: your

family, your friends, even your health. These things are temporal; kingdom work is eternal.

11. Go through every door God opens. If He didn't want you to go through them, He wouldn't be opening them.
12. Think twice about saying no to a Christian opportunity. If you do, feel guilty, *really* guilty.
13. Read the Bible an hour a day. If you don't, you're not very spiritual.
14. Feel as if you have to pray for great blocks of time. That's how you know you're in fellowship with God.
15. Give up secular activities for church-related ones. Don't waste time on things that don't count.
16. You've been saved to serve, so get going.

When I finished verbalizing my last maxim, I slipped the list to my husband. "Give me your thoughts," I requested, wondering whether he would laugh or cry.

He did neither. But he was serious as his eyes studied the page. When he finished contemplating the last pressure-message, he looked up, caught my eye, and flatly stated, "You've done all these things yourself, you know. You're trying to care for the whole world and still take care of yourself."

I realized then I *had* to write the book. And it would be for *me*.

Acknowledgments

A special thanks goes to the following individuals, who cared enough to render "above and beyond" help:

to Lee for his loving support and tireless effort from the beginning to the end of this project;

to Traci for the idea for this book;

to Charette for suggestions as to how the material should be presented;

to Lee, El, Judy, Nancy, and Laurie for evaluating and sharpening my ideas;

to Kyra and Lee for typing and retyping the manuscript;

to Patsy for writing a beautiful foreword;

to Janis for her enthusiastic, balanced channeling of my efforts;

to the team at Broadman and Holman for contributing finishing touches;

and to everybody who prayed.

Also, I wish to thank the friends, acquaintances, and seminar participants who inspired the following pages. While some dialogues, conversations, and incidents are, of necessity, composites, the personal illustrations are not. They happened as recorded (as best I can remember). I am grateful, however, for every contribution, large or small. Thank you, friends, and thank You, Heavenly Father.

Introduction

"Mommy, Mommy, come quick!
Valerie and Mark are wrecking my puzzle."

Laurie dropped her spoon, turned down the stove, grabbed a dish towel, and raced for the den, wiping her hands along the way.

As she ran, she heard an upstairs door slam, followed by muffled giggles.

When she entered the room, her heart stopped. She knew how hard Jessica had been working to assemble her new Snow White puzzle, a treasured birthday present. A few minutes ago the project had been near completion.

Now there was her daughter, sitting on the den floor, reaching for the puzzle's scattered pieces. She was sobbing. On the game table beside her was the Disney figure, now looking rather disjointed. The pretty face was resting by itself at the corner of the table. A right arm had been torn from its shoulder. And a slipper was lying on top of the maiden's vest.

Laurie bounded upstairs. The giggling stopped. When she came back down, she gathered her daughter in her arms and held her tightly. Then together, the two began to reassemble the broken puzzle. As the last piece slipped into place, Jessica hugged her mother.

"Thanks, Mom," she said. "Snow White's back together again."

Laurie returned to the kitchen to resume dinner preparations. But she had a hard time concentrating. Her mind was still in the den, reviewing the image of the fractured figure.

That night she had a dream. As the scene in her reverie came alive, she was standing on the stairs overlooking the game table in the den.

Crowding around it were familiar figures: family, friends, her boss, a community leader, and a pastor from her local church. Light from the fireplace was playing across their features.

She spotted the object of their attention: an enlarged photograph of herself lying on the table. One of her favorites, it was a full-figure shot, posed beside a flowering pear tree. She liked the fact she looked "all put together."

Soon her eyes were drawn to the corner of the room near the mantel. There, lurking in the shadows was someone she felt she should know. But she had a hard time placing him. As she studied his body language, her unrest grew.

Suddenly he whipped from his pocket a pair of scissors, the blades flashing in the flickering light. Laurie felt her muscles tighten. What was this stranger going to do?

Reaching out of the shadows, he passed the scissors to her husband. Her husband took them, leaned for the photograph, snipped a portion, and kept it.

"I can't believe this!" Laurie declared.

Then her husband passed both the scissors and the photograph to one of her friends. Her friend then snipped and passed the photograph to her pastor, who, in turn, passed it on to the community leader. Her boss was next. Soon everyone was holding a fragment. The picture in its completeness no longer existed.

"The whole world wants a chunk of me," Laurie moaned, "and nobody seems to care how much it hurts. Why are they doing this? Why?

"Who's the mysterious initiator? How strange he looks as he emerges from the shadows.

"Uh-oh! He's coming toward me . . .

"He has the scissors . . .

"Help!"

Laurie bolted upright in bed. By this time she was wide awake. So was her husband. He was getting her a glass of water.

"You must have had a nightmare," he concluded as he leaned around the frame of the bathroom door.

"I did," she said. "It was awful."

"Well, it's over," he comforted, handing her the glass.

She received his gift gratefully, then paused to gaze into its contents.

"Yes," she repeated, "it's over."

But was it over? Really? Or would the whole world continue to make its demands? And would Laurie continue to try to meet them?

Part One

The Pressures
a Christian Woman Feels

[God's] voice will always be in harmony with itself, no matter in how many different ways he may speak. The voices may be many, the message can be but one. If God tells me in one voice to do or to leave undone anything, he cannot possibly tell me the opposite in another voice. If there is a contradiction in the voices, the speakers cannot be the same. Therefore my rule for distinguishing the voice of God would be to bring it to the test of this harmony.

—Hannah Whitall Smith[1]

*Some women say yes to the Lord
and no to the world.
Others say yes to the world
but no to the Lord. But the double-minded
woman says yes to everything.
—Annie Chapman[2]*

1

Meet Those Crying Needs!

"Choose for yourselves today whom you will serve."
Joshua 24:15, NASB

Call us FCWs, short for Fractured Christian Women.

We're doing more than we should, yet feeling guilty we're not doing even more. Because we are serious about our faith, we really want our lives to count. But there are even more demands on Christians than on secular super-moms. And the demands are killing us.

It isn't easy being a woman, a wife, a mother, and a career person. It isn't easy coming home from work exhausted, having to straighten up the house, do the wash, pick up the kids, throw a meal together, run off to a church meeting, and then appear lovely and enticing to one's husband—especially when one is feeling frantic, frazzled, fragmented, and fractured—and unable to get free.

Everybody wants part of us, and nobody seems to care if we get torn as each grabs for a share. Each time someone takes a chunk, we wince in pain. We yearn for the wholeness brought to Snow White. But who will do the honors for us? We can't turn to our families, to our friends, or even to our church, for they are all part of the fracturing process.

"Meet my needs!" the world is screaming. And most needs are legitimate; some are even praiseworthy. But whose needs should come first? And where do our personal needs come in? Can *no* ever be a sanctified word, especially in Christian service? Can we even think such a thing without feeling guilty?

Somewhere along the line we have come to believe a good Christian is expected to seize every church-approved opportunity that presents itself, for it is our involvement that advances the kingdom of God. So we do, do, do until we can do no more.

At times, of course, we suspect, "Something's wrong here." But before we can troubleshoot the problem, we hear a sermon entitled "Burn Out for God!" Feeling guilty, we volunteer to chair the outreach program that we've been turning down for months. However, in order to do the job, we will have to sacrifice something important. But sacrifice is what the Christian life is all about, isn't it? Or is it?

We know we need help, but where do we go? Ah! A support group is forming at church. A meeting for stressed-out women. What an answer to prayer. The only problem is that the group is to meet on Thursday evening at 8:00. We remember we already have something scheduled on Thursdays at 8:00.

Our brains flash "Overload!"

Then it dawns on us: "In order to receive help dealing with those activities I'm already committed to, I will have to commit to yet another one!"

"I don't need this!" we scream. "How did I get so far off track?"

The answer may lie in what we are hearing from those around us.

The messages we are receiving may or may not be the same as those the world is sending us. But does that matter? What we are hearing is what we are hearing, and it is fragmenting us.

Listen to the Many Voices

* *Our husbands:* "I have needs: physical, emotional, intellectual, and spiritual. As my helpmeet, you are expected to meet them. I should be number one in your life."

* *Our kids:* "We come first. And you, Mom, are our primary caregiver. So give us everything you've got—and then some. You don't want us to turn out bad, do you?"

* *Our parents:* "We're getting older, you know. We'll be needing you more and more as time goes on. Don't forget us."

* *Our friends:* "Stop by when you get a chance. I miss our chats over coffee."

* *Our neighbors:* "We'd like to get to know you, but you're

hardly ever home. Maybe one of these days we can get together."

* *Our jobs:* "Produce or you're fired. This is no place for people who can't work overtime. Remember, you need this job."

* *Our communities:* "If you're going to live in our neighborhood, you should give something in return. Collecting for this charity should only take a couple of hours. Okay?"

* *Our Christian role models:* "We're successful in our ministries. How is your ministry going?"

* *Our churches:* "Saved to Serve. That's our motto. We'll keep you busy every night of the week. Here are just a few of our needs:
  - The office: 'We need typists.'
  - The youth program: 'We need sponsors.'
  - The choir: 'We need altos.'
  - The education committee: 'We need teachers.'
  - The mission board: 'We need homes.'
  - The finance committee: 'We need counters.'
  - The women's society: 'We need circle leaders.'
  - The visitation committee: 'We need volunteers.'
  - The property committee: 'We need painters.'
  - The hospitality committee: 'We need refreshments.'
  - The worship committee: 'We need ushers.'"

* *Our souls:* "Why are you neglecting me? After all, I am the real you, the source from which your service to others flows. Ignore me, and I shrivel. But refresh me with a quiet moment in the Word of God, and I take on new life. I will heal you, help you reassess your goals, encourage you to rearrange your priorities and restore your passion for living. In fact, if you fill me with good stuff, I'll overflow with blessing into the lives of those you love. But I need nourishment. And I need it regularly."

All voices in unison: "Meet our needs!"

Our response: "I hear you. But when is enough? I have needs, too. Where do they come in? Do I, as a person, count?"

A Lone Voice: "Of course you do. If you listened only to Me, you would know that. But you are listening to everybody but Me. No wonder you are confused."

Accentuating the Positive

As I was gathering my notes at the end of a message on pressures that are fracturing women, I noticed an attractive young woman pushing through the crowd toward me. When she finally reached the podium, she patiently waited her turn, then blurted, "I'm Teddie. Can we talk?"

"Sure," I agreed, hoping she would offer some additional enlightenment to the topic I had just addressed.

"You were describing me today," she began. "I have experienced every frustration you mentioned. I am the Fractured Christian Woman to the extreme. I hear those same driving voices. But I must say, even though I do not agree with the totality of their messages, I do agree with much of what they are saying. For example, next to God, a husband should be the most important person in a married woman's life. Kids do need to be reared in the nurture and admonition of the Lord! And we do have an obligation to see that the needs of our aging parents are met."

"Definitely," I agreed.

"And," Teddie continued, "we should strive to do our best—whether it's working in an office, being a friend or neighbor, or becoming involved as a good citizen of our respective communities. But not at the expense of church involvement. After all, anybody can do secular jobs, but only Christians can do the Lord's work."

"Amen!" I agreed.

"And whatever we do, either inside or outside the home or the church, it must be done as a tribute to the God who created us. We both agree on these things.

"But what bothered me," Teddie pressed, "was when you mentioned it's possible to do all these things, even church work, and neglect your own soul. I never thought of it that way before. But I know now, in my attempt to balance priorities, my spiritual life has come up short. I think you've hit on my biggest problem."

"That's the biggest problem for most of us, Teddie. You're no different. Most of us just don't want to admit it. Would you be able to spend an hour or so discussing further the pressures Christian women are under? Maybe together we can separate truth from overstatement and put our souls back on the top of our list of priorities."

"Sounds good to me," Teddie replied. And as we talked, certain truths became clear to both of us.

Overstatement and Truth

* *The FCW thinks*, "My job as a Christian wife is to meet my

husband's every need."

The Lone Voice whispers, "Really? Is it not God's job to meet every need? For you to even try will cause fracturing."

* *The FCW thinks*, "My kids need me more than my husband does."

The Lone Voice whispers, "Not so. Although your children do have needs, their needs are not more important than your husband's. To think so is to risk your marriage."

* *The FCW thinks*, "I foresee the day when I may have to care for my parents at the expense of my immediate family."

The Lone Voice whispers, "Not at the expense of your immediate family. The needs of your parents come after the needs of your family, unless, of course, the parental need is urgent. Then you should meet it as expeditiously as possible and turn your attention back to your immediate family."

* *The FCW thinks*, "A good friend 'jumps' whenever her friends say 'Jump!'"

The Lone Voice whispers, "Careful. A good friend meets her own needs first. Then she has something to give to her friendship with others."

* *The FCW thinks*, "It's okay for my job to steal time from family activities because, in the long run, my family will benefit."

The Lone Voice whispers, "Although there are times when your job will take you away from your family, a job-first mindset could destroy your home. Remember, people are more important than things."

* *The FCW thinks*, "Community involvement is a necessary evil."

The Lone Voice whispers, "Not always. Think of the good that can come from working with your neighbors for a worthwhile goal, including an opportunity to share your faith."

* *The FCW thinks*, "God wants me to be as successful as my role models are."

The Lone Voice whispers, "Be yourself, serving in your own unique way. Success in God's eyes is not measured by outward results but by the inner movings of His Spirit."

* *The FCW thinks*, "I've been saved to serve my church."

The Lone Voice whispers, "You have been saved to glorify God. This may or may not involve service within the church. It is easy to equate glorifying God with doing church work. But this causes ministries to come before relationships and 'doing' before 'being.' The result is fracturing."

* *The FCW thinks*, "My soul is separate from the rest of me. Therefore, I can neglect it, and nobody will know the difference."

The Lone Voice whispers, "Your soul is an integral part of you, influencing your body, your intellect, your emotions, and your will. To neglect it is to neglect your source of power. And that will show."

Is it possible, then, that what Christians are interpreting as God's message may not be from God at all? That the get-out-there-and-do pressure we feel is from our families, our friends, our churches, even ourselves? But that it may not be from God at all?

Let's take a spiritual inventory:

- Are my efforts to please others pleasing God?
- If I were successful in meeting the needs of the whole world, would I necessarily be glorifying God?
- Am I wise in sacrificing secular activities for sacred ones?
- What is church work, anyway?
- What steps can I take to start reassembling the scattered pieces of my life?

A Divine Perspective

As I was reading in the Old Testament book of Isaiah, I came upon the following verse: "[God] sits enthroned above the circle of the earth, and its people are like grasshoppers" (Isa. 40:22).

Now, I've been called a lot of things in my life, but never a grasshopper. Time for some research, I decided.

So I buried myself in the encyclopedia. And, I must admit, most of what I read did not enlighten me. But three facts did.

First, grasshoppers hop (astounding, wouldn't you say?). These active little creatures have the capacity to jump twenty times their length. This translates into human leaps of forty yards, I discovered. No small feat!

I put the book down and thought for a moment. Yes, I confirmed, grasshoppers do hop. They hop to work, to the supermarket, to the mall, and to church. Boy, do they hop to church! They hop to morning service, evening service, midweek service, Sunday school, mission board, choir practice. You name it, they hop there.

Second, I learned that grasshoppers spit, especially when

handled roughly. And what comes out of their mouths is not very sweet. Tobacco juice, it is called. Even those that like to sing also spit. (Sorry about that, choir members.)

Third, I studied the grasshopper's vision. Like other insects, it has compound eyes, enabling it to see in several different directions, especially forward. I identified, for I like to think I have forward vision too.

But then I learned grasshoppers can also see behind them—without moving their heads. *Neat,* I thought. While sitting in church, I could observe who comes in late and sneaks into the back pew, and I myself would still be facing piously to the front. Quite an advantage!

Grasshoppers can also see sideways—again without moving their heads. What a boon to a mother with kids strung out down the pew. If one acted up, she could spot the troublemaker quickly. And if she couldn't reach him, she could just turn her head and spit. A creative method of church discipline, wouldn't you say?

But one way grasshoppers cannot see is up. Their vision is limited to the horizontal. Not only that, but with their sectional lenses, they have difficulty focusing even on what's up close.

No wonder God calls us grasshoppers! Frantic little creatures we are, hopping from blade of grass to blade of grass, thinking our world of activity is all there is. How tragic to be missing the vertical view, the one that leads to wholeness!

What Can We Do to Change Things?

Vow to put God first. "You're number one, Lord, now, tomorrow, and always." By expressing our commitment in a formal way, we're acknowledging a rite of passage. Our intention is to go in a new direction, and we want it to be known. No more vacillating. From now on, the Lord is in top place.

Make sure Hubby knows he's right behind God in our list of priorities. Here's a chance to be creative. Schedule regular dates. Take time to rub his shoulders, fold his laundry, or set aside an hour just to talk.

An effective way to teach children what a good marriage is, counselors tell us, is by role modeling affection for Dad. "Kids, we had a marriage before we had you," we may tell them. "And we hope to have a marriage long after you are gone. Right now you are important, extremely important, but not more important than your father."

Give our children a sense of security. We can tell our children this: "We mothers are biologically created by God to be your primary caregivers, kids. And we are committed to doing our best. But we are not your only caregivers." (In fact, most kids have fathers, relatives, and siblings.) "Each family member has something to contribute to your growth. So when Mommy can't be here, there will be others to take up the slack. And when times of loneliness come, remember your heavenly Father. He's the most important Caregiver of all. And He never goes away."

See that our parents are loved and cared for in a way that honors God and respects the needs of our immediate families. We of the "sandwich generation" owe a lot to those who graciously gave to us. But does this mean we have to be primary caregivers, especially when such care interferes with the running of our immediate families?

"Lord, the decisions we face are agonizing. Help us to make them with the interests of our husbands and children in mind. When we lose our parents, we don't want to find we've lost other loved ones as well."

Schedule fellowship times with friends and neighbors. If we don't plan to reach out, we probably won't. But if we pencil names on our calendars, sharing *will* take place. In the process, we'll be reaffirming the biblical teaching that investments in people pay rich dividends.

Periodically reassess our job situation. Every once in a while it's good to take an inventory. After all, things change, so we must periodically ask ourselves these questions:

- Do I really need to work outside the home?
- Is my work interfering with my family life? my church life? my personal life? the nourishment of my soul?
- If so, what can I do about it?

Accept, but limit, community service.. We want to do our part to contribute to those around us. But we don't want our community involvement to be an I-have-to-do-this bondage. Perhaps one or two "collections" a year will suffice. By going door-to-door we'll be introducing ourselves to folks we may meet no other way. And the rewards could be eternal!

Observe how other Christians minister, but without personal intimidation. It's easy to get caught in the comparison trap and miss God's plan for us as unique individuals. A detached observance of others will enable us to select the good we can incorporate into our own ministries and discard what we can't. We're then free to be God's one-of-a-kind representative.

Seek to discover a "ministry niche" within the church. Everybody has an opportunity to do something: teach, sing, type, organize, visit, bake, whatever. What do you think would happen if, in our larger congregations, we adopted the slogan, "All involved, but none overinvolved"? Would not our churches come alive with efficiency? Would not all bases be covered, all needs met? Instead of being hampered by a system in which 10 percent of the people do 90 percent of the work, perhaps halfheartedly at times, would we not have 100 percent of the people involved, each doing one thing well? And wouldn't that make a difference?

Schedule spiritual refueling stops, reserved for Bible study and prayer. Friends, we are running on fumes. It's time to fill up, to let our source of power overflow, even to catch some extra to hold in reserve. For how are we going to meet the needs of a world of fellow travelers, if we have nothing left to give?

Confirmation from God's Word

1. Read Proverbs 31:10–31 describing the virtuous woman.

2. Is the Virtuous Woman real or an ideal? How do we know?

3. List the various responsibilities the virtuous woman is committed to.

- Does she accomplish all these tasks by herself, or does she have help (see v. 15)?

4. What adjectives can we use to describe her?

- How many of these adjectives relate to her works (v. 31)? How many to her "character" (v. 10)?
- On which does her worth (v. 10) depend: character or works? Why?
- How does character affect works?
- Do works, especially too many, affect character? How?

5. How does the fact that the virtuous woman puts God first (v. 30) affect her relationship with her husband (v. 28)? her children (v. 28)? her community (v. 20)?

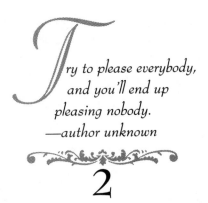

*ry to please everybody,
and you'll end up
pleasing nobody.*
—author unknown

2

Be a People Pleaser!

*Crowds of people came to hear him and to be healed of their sicknesses.
But Jesus often withdrew to lonely places and prayed.*
Luke 5:15–16

It was Saturday morning. I had decided that since my husband would be away the entire weekend, the kids could use a special treat. So on Friday evening after they had gone to bed, I made and refrigerated gingerbread dough. I was hoping their favorite TV programs the next morning would keep them occupied until I finished my project.

After removing the dough from the refrigerator, I floured the cutting board, rolling pin, and cookie cutter generously. Then I patted the wad of dough, rolled it out, and with my cutter shaped as many men as possible.

"Phew!" I sighed. "They all look the same."

Slipping the spatula under one figure at a time, I transferred my creations to a well-greased cookie sheet. As the oven was heating, I pressed raisins into each figure to represent eyes, nose, mouth, and buttons. Cute!

When the oven reached the proper temperature, I slid the sheet of men onto the rack and watched through the glass as the figures puffed out their chests.

Shortly the timer rang. As I opened the door and removed the cookie sheet, I admired my work.

"They're adorable!" I concluded. Then with horror I noticed

that as hard as I had tried for uniformity, the cookies were not all the same. One was browner, another thicker, a third had fatter raisins, and—my word—one had an extra button! How could that have happened?

"Easily," a voice within me reasoned. "Think of all the variables in the baking process. There's the rolling of the dough, the positioning of the figures in the oven, the size of the raisins, and the biggest variable of all, you! Therefore, uniformity in cookie making is impossible."

The voice continued, "It is in people-pleasing too. Aren't you burdening yourself unduly by thinking if you treat everybody with the same tender, loving care, they'll all respond the way you want them to? Each person is not only a unique blend of ingredients, but each reacts differently to the heat and pressures of life. Remember this as you weigh what you hear them say to you. And be tolerant of what has shaped them—factors unknown to you."

Listen to the Many Voices

* "Strive to be a people-pleaser. How people respond to you shows how effective you are in manifesting the love of Christ."

* "Be available whenever people need you. This is the way to please them."

* "It is more important to minister to the soul than to the body. So concentrate on the spiritual."

* "It is more important to minister to the body than to the soul. So concentrate on the physical."

* "Put others before yourself. When you give to others, you receive blessings in return."

* "Treat everybody the same. Then nobody can accuse you of partiality."

* "Don't offend anyone. Your offense could keep a soul from entering the kingdom of God."

All voices in unison: "Be all things to all people all the time. That's how you show God's love."

Our response: "I try, but I can't even live up to my own expectations, let alone God's. Does this mean I'm beyond help?"

A Lone Voice: "No, but in order to get help, you must sort out My voice from all the others. For My voice is the only one that counts."

Accentuating the Positive

I was holding the phone on my shoulder as I sliced tomatoes for a salad. The voice on the line belonged to Cathy, who was usually exuberant about her new faith in Christ. Today, however, she was anxious about the pressure she was under to be a people-pleaser. My ears perked up.

As she poured out her frustration, I realized it was similar to mine—with one exception. Cathy was maintaining a positive attitude and wanted to share it. "You know, Peg," she continued, "wanting to please is not all bad."

"How's that?" I queried.

"Well," Cathy responded, "it is commendable to want people to like us—to let them know we're genuinely interested in them. Of course, that means we have to be available when they need us, even to the point of personal inconvenience, I guess."

"That's true," I agreed. "But sometimes I have a hard time sorting out which needs are more important: physical or spiritual. Jesus met both. And often He used the physical to open the door to the spiritual."

Cathy was quiet for a moment. Then she said, "I never connected spiritual and physical needs before, but now that I think about it, God reached me through such a connection. The day my husband had his accident, a woman I didn't even know brought a casserole to the house. I was so moved, I listened intently as she talked about her Lord. This was the first in a series of events that resulted in my becoming a Christian."

"I love it!" I exclaimed. "But kindness works in reverse, too. Did you ever notice that when you reach out to others, you yourself end up getting blessed?"

"I have noticed that. Uh-oh! My kids just walked in and they're starved. I'm afraid I have to go."

"I understand," I empathized. "But before you go, let me thank you. You just contributed to a book I'm writing."

"Uh-oh!" Cathy said again, this time teasingly. Then she hung up.

As I opened the door to the fridge and slid the salad inside, I thought, "Cathy has such a positive attitude toward life. She would be a good one to help me sort out what is overstatement in the area of people-pleasing.

I suggested it and she agreed. So at a later date the two of us examined the pressure-messages we are all hearing.

Overstatement and Truth

* *The FCW thinks*, "If what I do does not please others, the fault must lie with me. I must be an ineffective communicator of Christ's love."

The Lone Voice whispers, "Not necessarily so. Others have responsibility too—for their reactions to your actions. So learn to do your best, leave reactions to God, and keep on serving."

* *The FCW thinks*, "I'm fractured because I'm doing too much. I'll give up ministering to those whose needs are physical to concentrate on the spiritual."

The Lone Voice whispers, "An unwise decision. Physical needs can be doors to spiritual ones. Besides, God cares for the whole person."

* *The FCW thinks*, "One way to please others is to give them what they need when they need it."

The Lone Voice whispers, "Careful! This mindset creates situations in which no matter how much you do, it is never 'enough.'"

* *The FCW thinks*, "The ideal Christian woman says no to her own needs in order to say yes to the needs of others, for others must always come first."

The Lone Voice whispers, "Always? A wise Christian woman makes time for herself. Otherwise, she will be in no position to give to the others in her life. Even Christ came apart from the crowds, to fill up before giving out (see Luke 5:15–16). To do this He had to leave many needs unmet, at least temporarily."

* *The FCW thinks*, "I must make an effort to like everyone I meet because that's how to show Christian love."

The Lone Voice whispers, "You are equating 'like' to 'love.' They are not necessarily the same. Love is like a patchwork quilt in the process of being assembled. As random patches of color wait to be joined, some shades naturally go together, while others scream, 'Separate us! We clash.' While there is a place for all the squares, it is not necessarily side by side. A wise Designer knows this, joining only those that complement each other. Wise patches let Him—and appreciate their positioning."

* *The FCW thinks*, "When I reach out in love, I should be able to avoid offending people."

The Lone Voice whispers, "Impossible! There are people who will take offense regardless of your approach. Some are tired; others are dissatisfied with life. And there are a few who are actually looking for opportunities to lash out in anger. Besides, the message of the cross carries its own offense. So wrap the gospel as attractively as possible, but realize some will throw the gift back in your face. It happened to the Savior, too."

A Divine Perspective

In order to get a heavenly view on the subject of people-pleasing, I decided to turn to that passage of Scripture known as the Hall of Faith, Hebrews 11. I chose it because it highlights the lives of Old Testament saints who are examples for believers today, including me.

As I read, I embellished each name with facts I remembered from the fuller accounts in Genesis and Exodus. I was able to recall enough details to realize here were people who, for the most part, had chosen to please God with their lives. Submission to His will, however, often resulted in their displeasing others. When they did choose to please others at the expense of God's will, the results were painful. Yet all these people were being cited for their faith. There was much to learn from their examples, I deduced.

First, I studied Noah, whose peers laughed in derision as he assembled the ark God had commanded him to build. ("How stupid can you get, Noah? We've never had a flood!") When the rains finally came, though, and the mockers were drowned, who was laughing then? I wondered. Whose responses counted in the long run: man's or God's?

The answers came. God honored Noah by naming him "an heir of righteousness that comes by faith" (v. 7). "Lord, make me as worthy an heir as Noah was," I found myself praying.

Still thinking of heirs, I read of Sarah, a beautiful Hebrew woman, who was driven to desperation by her desire to conceive a child. After all, God had promised heirs as numerous as the stars. But it wasn't happening. So why not help God along?

"Maybe Hagar, my maid, can conceive a child for me," Sarah thought. "If I offer her to Abraham, he will be pleased. So will I.

So will God."

As we know, Hagar did conceive, and Sarah's husband Abraham was pleased. So was Sarah—temporarily. But one day reality struck. As Sarah stared at Hagar's expanding waistline, then looked down at her own flat tummy, jealousy consumed her. She lashed out at the servant girl, who ended up fleeing for her life.

These shenanigans must have both angered and disappointed God, for He repeated His original promise to the barren couple. The heir was to come through Sarah!

"You're kidding, Lord! I'm now ninety years old," I imagined Sarah saying. "You're not going to open my womb at this age! Ouch!" But God did. Nine months later Isaac was born. Ouch again!

As a woman, I found myself empathizing with Sarah's pain, both before and after the birth. But I was reminded afresh there is no place in the Christian life for the manipulation of people or circumstances, even when, as in this case, the goal is to accomplish God's plan. "Forgive me, Lord," I prayed, "for the times I too have interfered with Your divine design. And keep me from doing it again."

Then I read of Jacob, the son of a father with failing eyesight and a mother with a conniving heart. Both wanted to be pleased. Jacob was caught in the middle.

"Pretend you are your brother," Rebekah advised her son. "Then your father will give your brother's blessing to you instead of to him."

Flat-out deceit. That's what this was. Jacob knew it, but in his desire to please his mother, he decided to go ahead with the scheme.

The ruse worked. Jacob did receive his father Isaac's blessing. But when Isaac realized he had been betrayed, he "trembled violently," the Bible says (Gen. 27:33). Rebekah trembled, too, as she watched her favorite son leave home to escape his brother's wrath. What a price to pay for a blessing!

I brightened as I read of Joseph, who had refused to allow himself to be seduced by Potiphar's wife. Here was a young man, far away from home, with physical bliss at his fingertips. Who would ever know?

Joseph, however, refused to be compromised. But his refusal so angered Potiphar's wife that she had him sent to prison, a high price tag for moral purity. But Joseph was at peace. He had been true to God's principles, and His Father in heaven was pleased. In fact, because of his stand, "the Lord was with Joseph," we read, "and gave him success in whatever he did" (Gen. 39:23). Oh, for the courage to be firm whatever the cost!

Next, I read of Moses, a humble Hebrew reared in an Egyptian palace. His beginnings had been as traumatic as beginnings get: after all, in an attempt to save her baby's life, his mother had placed him in a basket in the crocodile-infested Nile River. In the providence of God, however, Pharaoh's daughter found him and hired his own mother to nurture him. She must have done a good job because when Moses faced the grown-up choice of declaring himself a Hebrew or an Egyptian, he didn't hesitate. "He chose to be mistreated along with the people of God rather than to enjoy the pleasures of sin for a short time," we are told (Heb. 11:25). His decision, however, angered his foster father so much that Pharoah tried to kill him. Here's another person willing to pay the price of not pleasing people, I noted.

The list continued to challenge me. "Others [in God's service]," I was reminded, "were tortured, jeered, flogged, chained, imprisoned, stoned, sawed in two, and put to death by the sword" (see vv. 36–37). Yet these were all "commended for their faith" (v. 39). I want to be commended too, I decided.

As I read into the next chapter, I pictured a "great cloud of witnesses" (Heb. 12:1), people who made it through life and are now cheering us on from heaven. I pictured Noah, Sarah, Joseph, and Moses in the bleachers exhorting me. "You can make it too, Peg," they seemed to be shouting. "Just stop trying to be a people-pleaser. Keep your eyes only on God. And don't be discouraged if you make a mistake. There are lots of new beginnings in God's grace."

As I read on, God's grace became very real to me. I saw Jesus, the Savior, in the throes of death. Lifted up, surrounded by mockers, alone, naked, "despising his shame," He was hanging there—arms outstretched—for me. I knew what brought Him to this place. He had refused to please the religious leaders. Now He was being subjected to one of the cruelest punishments devised by man: crucifixion.

Help was at His fingertips. I knew that. He could have commanded angels to reclothe Him or to pull the nails from His wrists. He could have asked the Father to vindicate Him with a heavenly pronouncement of His innocence. But He did none of these things. Instead, He chose to endure the pain because that was the will of His Father. "Consider Him Who endured such opposition from sinful men," the passage reminds us, "so that you will not grow weary and lose heart" (Heb. 12:3).

All these role models, singled out by God, faced decisions concerning relationships. Some chose well; others, poorly. Those who chose poorly paid a price. Those who chose well paid, too, but their price was worth it. They were pleasing God. And God set "joy" before them.

As these Scripture verses pierced my heart, I found myself wanting to be in God's contemporary Hall of Faith. I knew, though, I would have to make some changes in order to accomplish my goal.

What Can We Do to Change Things?

Give up trying to be all things to all people all the time. What may appear to be pressure from others ("People expect this from me, so I had better perform") may, in fact, be pressure from ourselves ("I want people to like me, so I had better please them"). If there is to be a burden, may it come from God, for His burden is easy to bear (see Matt. 11:29).

Study the life of Christ for examples of divine restraint. One time as I was reading the gospels, I decided to be creative. This time I would concentrate not on what the Savior did but on what He didn't do, not the times He served but the times He didn't serve, not the needs He met but the needs He didn't meet. And did I get blessed! I pictured each scene, trying to imagine how the Savior's restraint might have affected those who did not receive the help they were expecting.

As I got deeper into my study, it became increasingly clear that Christ was living exclusively to please His Father: "I have come to do your will, O God" (Heb. 10:7). To the Savior, the approval of people was secondary.

In order to structure an effective ministry, it appeared He

established a Pyramid of People Priorities. This enabled Him to say no to those at the bottom in order to say yes to those at the top— and to do so without guilt. And even though those at the top were fewer in number (sometimes just one person), He made a greater personal investment in them than He did in the larger groups at the bottom. I found this refreshing.

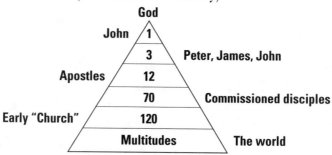

Christ's Pyramid of People Priorities
(A Controlled Ministry)

But His investment in lives did not always turn out positively, I was reminded. One of His twelve disciples (those in whom He had poured three years of Himself) turned out to have a traitor's heart and, in time, betrayed His Lord. Perhaps we could paraphrase P. T. Barnum and say, "You can please all of the people some of the time and some of the people all of the time, but you can't please all of the people all of the time." Not even Christ could do that!

From the circle of twelve, three became Jesus' best friends: Peter, James, and John. His relationship with them probably rivaled His friendship with Mary, Martha, and Lazarus, I decided, who also were precious companions. The three disciples, though, must have been special, for they were privileged to view wonders no one else saw (the Transfiguration, for example), hear things reserved for their ears alone ("Don't tell anyone"), and accompany the Master to places denied the rest ("Jesus . . . led them up a high mountain by themselves," Matt. 17:1). No doubt jealousy surfaced in those disciples who were excluded, I imagined. But Jesus knew what He was about, so He continued conducting a selective ministry anyway.

He even chose one disciple from these three to be His closest companion of all. John, the beloved, he was called. In this relationship there were probably even deeper truths probed, greater love shared, more spiritual intimacies exchanged, I guessed. What a relief to know Jesus didn't treat everybody equally!

But what, besides selectivity, made the ministry of Christ an effective one? I asked myself. The answer came: control. He controlled when, where, how, and to whom He ministered. He realized that if He did not control His outreach, it would end up controlling Him. Then nobody at all would benefit fully.

So His was a ministry to some at the exclusion of others. It could be no other way. And in the end, it paid off. For it was not the multitudes that penetrated the world with the gospel; it was the few. It is the same today, I realized.

Another contributing factor to the effectiveness of Christ's ministry, I discovered, was planned withdrawal. He would temporarily halt his teaching and healing ministry for times of personal renewal. He felt the need to get away, not only from the pressing crowds but from the disciples as well. Such withdrawal must have raised eyebrows ("Jesus doesn't like our company"), but this was the cost of obedience. He was out to do the Father's will, no matter what! I found these concepts refreshingly convicting.

Establish a personal Pyramid of People Priorities, *modeling it after the Savior's.* Like Christ, we want to make sure God the Father is first. Our relationship with Him will then generate the spiritual energy we need to minister to the others farther down our pyramids. .

My Pyramid of People Priorities
(A Controlled Ministry)

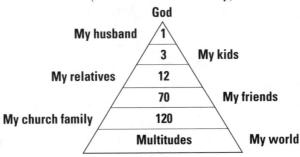

Who comes next and the order in which their names appear will depend, of course, upon what God tells us individually to do. A possible arrangement is suggested. For marrieds, one's spouse comes high on the list followed by children. For singles, a best friend or close relative may be placed in the top slot; children will be left out altogether for non-parents. Positioning church members in relationship to non-believers will vary according to the relationship, but as a general rule of ministry, the Bible says, "Therefore, as we have opportunity, let us do good to all people, especially to those who belong to the family of believers (Gal. 6:10).

This positioning will serve to give needed structure to our relationships. Not that our established order can't be flexible. Indeed, it must be (except for God's position, of course)! But how reassuring to have a biblical basis for saying no to some very pressing voices.

Now to some unsettling questions. What happens if we intentionally rearrange our order? For example, what if we choose to spend more time with church members than we do with family? Or if we place the needs of our kids before the needs of our husbands? Or if the world is allowed to usurp our quiet time with God? Hopefully, danger signals will flash, getting our attention. Something is wrong with our priorities and we must make some changes.

If, on the other hand, we say no to a community project to spend time at church or no to a church meeting to spend time with the kids, we are sending positive messages to those we care about most. In the process, those neglected may react negatively. But if God is pleased, do the others really matter?

There will be times, of course, when out of necessity, our listing must be allowed to rearrange itself. A sick child, for example, will take undisputed precedence over a healthy husband. A spiritually receptive neighbor, who is actively seeking answers, may shoot right to the top of the pyramid. And an important series of meetings at church may require us to drop everything else temporarily in order to be part of the blessing. While these involvements may totally consume us for awhile, it is comforting to have a workable structure to fall back into when the "crisis" is over.

Be sensitive to hearts that are hurting. "Please handle me with care," fragile personalities plead. And we try. But now and then we foul up. We can't help it. We'll reach out to someone who prefers to be left alone, or we'll accidentally "drop" the too heavy spirits of someone we never should have tried to lift. It's hard to win at this game of people-pleasing. But who said we are supposed to?

Be the first to say "I'm sorry." Scripture calls for Christians to go the extra mile. That means initiating the process of reconciliation. When we do this, we are pleasing God. For Jesus said, "If you are offering your gift at the altar and there remember your brother has something against you . . . go and be reconciled to your brother; then come and offer your gift" (Matt. 5:25–26).

Trying to right a wrong, however, offers no guarantee of success. After all, it takes two to reconcile. But even if our efforts are rebuffed, we can rest in the knowledge we have tried. Our obedience to the Word of God has served to set us free—free to "shake the dust off our feet" and find another place to minister where we are accepted. In fact, this is what Christians are commanded to do (see Matt. 10:14).

Confirmation from God's Word

1. Read Mark 3:1–12 about the healing of the withered hand and Christ's withdrawal from the crowd.
2. List the various pressures Jesus faced in these verses.
3. Make note of how He handled each pressure.
4. Ponder:
    - Did Jesus please the Pharisees when He healed the man with the shriveled hand?
    - Did Jesus please the crowd when He took refuge in a small boat?
    - Do you think Jesus pleased God in these same instances? On what do you base your answer?

aid the Robin to the Sparrow
"I should really
like to know
Why these anxious human beings
Rush about and worry so."
Said the Sparrow to the Robin
"Friend, I think that it must be
That they have no heavenly Father
Such as cares for you and me."
—Elizabeth Cheney, *"Overheard in an Orchard"*

3

Put Others Before Yourself!

Thou wilt show me the path of life: in thy presence is fullness of joy;
at thy right hand there are pleasures forevermore.
Psalm 16:11, KJV

The alarm went off, jolting Katie out of a sound sleep. She groped for the turn-off knob.

"It's morning," her brain registered. "That means I have to get up, get dressed, get breakfast, get the kids off to school, get my husband off to work, and get myself to the office. What else do I have to do today?"

She nudged her husband, who groaned. Then she sat up, swung her legs to the floor, felt for her slippers, threw on a robe, and shuffled to the bathroom. As she turned the faucet, she looked in the mirror.

"Some Christian I am," she sighed. "Where's the joy of living a new day for the Lord?"

One by one she awakened the kids. They were not exactly abounding with enthusiasm either.

Soon she was in the kitchen, lining up cereal boxes on the table. Then she went to the counter to pack lunches. She remembered to slip love notes, composed earlier (at a time when she could think), into the folded napkins. She wondered if they'd be found.

Then she turned around to see if everybody had made it to the table. They had.

"My husband looks serious," she thought. "No wonder. He has a hard day ahead.

"The kids haven't worked up any exuberance either. I'm not surprised. Peter has a test; Andrew faces tryouts for a class play; and Priscilla is nervous about beginning piano lessons."

When breakfast was over, the kids scattered. They ran first to the bathroom to clean their teeth, then to their rooms to pick up their book bags. Soon they were grabbing jackets from the hall closet and racing out the door—but not before kissing Mom and Dad good-bye.

Then it was her husband's turn to leave. He followed a similar procedure.

"This is no way to start the day," Katie sighed as she waved the last one off. "We're all rushing, everybody's tense, and nobody has any joy. What are we doing wrong?"

She returned to the kitchen, put back the cereal, refrigerated the milk, passed a damp sponge over the table, and ran to get dressed. Not much time to think.

Soon she was grabbing her coat, letting the dog out, and setting the locks on the door. Once in the garage, she slipped into her mini-van, started the ignition, and backed carefully into the driveway. In no time at all, she had joined the flow of traffic northward.

As she stopped at a light, she scanned the face of the driver to her left. He looked bored.

"Where's his joy?" she asked, shifting her foot to the accelerator as the light turned green.

By the time she swung into the parking lot at work, she realized she was on a treasure hunt, the treasure being joy, that fruit of the Spirit God promises to all who name His name. It seemed elusive.

She shut off the ignition, got out of the car, and locked the door. As she approached the entrance to her office building, she examined the faces of her fellow workers. Although most were friendly, few were displaying a genuine enthusiasm for living.

During lunch break, she decided to walk to the bank. No

joy there.

On the way home from work, she stopped at the supermarket to pick up a few things for dinner. The check-out lines were jammed. No joy there.

A run to school to pick up the kids didn't end the search either. Peter thought he could have done better on his test, and Andrew didn't get the part in the play he wanted. Katie tried to get them to dwell on the positive.

She used the same technique on Priscilla as she drove her to her first piano lesson. She felt only partially successful.

By the time she got through dinner and arrived at choir practice, she was sure she'd find an upbeat spirit. After all, this was church. If it were possible to find joy anywhere, it would be in the house of God. But she was wrong.

Granted, there were smiles as the choir members exchanged pleasantries, even a moment of hilarity as the basses boomed in too soon. But generally speaking, there seemed to be little time to enjoy life—or to enjoy each other enjoying life. There was too much work to be done.

On her way out of the church, Katie stuck her head in the door of the room where the missionary committee was planning the winter conference. Everybody looked serious. Then she peered into the teachers' meeting, and nobody even looked up.

"What is wrong?" Katie persisted. "Don't people take delight in living anymore?

"And what's wrong with me? I'm no better than anybody else I've been observing. I'm running so fast I'm just existing, not really experiencing much of anything. Where has my joy gone? What will it take to get it back?"

Listen to the Many Voices

* "Joy comes when you tend to your own needs after you have satisfied the needs of everybody else. To put yourself first is self-serving."

* "Keep pouring out, even when you feel there's nothing left to give. Life is not for quitters."

* "Be ready to take on that extra job. And be joyful about accepting when asked."

* "Smile all the time, and be liberal with your hugs. To become

spiritual, you have to get physical. Christians are known by their actions."

All voices in unison: "For the Christian, JOY is spelled 'Jesus, Others, then You.' And it is manifest in facial expression as well as in body language."

Our response: "I feel like a fake. I'm putting on a plastic smile, hugging people I don't feel like hugging and letting everyone else's needs run my life. And you're telling me this is joy?"

A Lone Voice: "Absolutely not. What you are describing is contrived Christianity. Genuine joy is eluding you because you are listening to too many voices. Listen only to Me because My voice is the only one that matters."

Accentuating the Positive

I was standing in the cashier's line of my favorite discount store. Suddenly I heard a familiar voice behind me. It belonged to Joanie, a friend who works as a receptionist in a local doctor's office.

"I've got just fifteen minutes to get back to work," Joanie said, checking her watch. "Think I'll make it?"

"Here," I gestured. "Step in front of me. I have only a manuscript to get back to."

"How's it going?" she asked.

"Okay, I guess, but I need some input from a fractured Christian woman."

"Meet your divine appointment!" Joanie exclaimed, stretching out her arms. Then holding up a furry stuffed dog, she asked, "Do you like this?"

"It's adorable," I answered, lifting its fur from its eyes. "Who's it for?"

"My mom," Joanie said. "Today's her birthday, and I'm just now getting her present. I'll swing by the care facility on the way home from work and drop it off. Of course, five minutes after I've gone, Mom won't know I've been there, but I do want to make her day special. Who knows how many more birthdays she'll have?"

"How do you feel about putting time and effort into an occasion that won't be remembered?"

"Wonderful!" Joanie enthused. "You can't give without receiving. In fact, what I receive will be far greater than anything I can give."

"I know what you mean. I guess it has to do with 'casting your bread on the waters.'"

"I know it does," Joanie chimed in. "Selflessness is the name of the game. By the way, did you see the Scripture reference in today's devotional? 'In humility consider others better than yourselves!' I just wish I could do more of that."

"Well, you're doing it today. You're reaching out to your mom at the expense of skipping your own lunch. And you already know your sacrifice probably won't even be appreciated."

"It will be when we all get to heaven," Joanie affirmed. "Right now is the 'enduring' time. Later is the time for rejoicing. I love the verse that says, 'For the joy that was set before Him, Jesus endured the cross.' Joy doesn't always come now, but it catches up with us eventually. That thought warms my heart.

"You know what else warms me?" Joanie asked as she moved forward and laid her animal on the counter. "Watching people do difficult tasks joyfully. That's the attitude I see in one of the nurses on Mom's floor. What a sweetheart she is! She's stressed out with more demands than she can possibly meet, yet she takes one at a time and does them with a smile. We could use more demonstrations of love like that!"

As she picked up her purchase, Joanie flashed an ear-to-ear smile. Then she reached out and hugged me. "Good talking with you," she said. Then with a wave she rushed out the door.

"Genuine joy is contagious," I concluded as I smiled at the cashier. "I wonder why everybody elses hugs don't affect me as positively as Joanie's just did? And why am I not as cheerful as she is?"

These questions caused me to look at the pressures Christian women are experiencing with the intent of sorting out the errors. At one point I called Joanie and used her as a sounding board.

Overstatement and Truth

* *The FCW thinks*, "Ministry to others is a source of joy, so I should feel good even when I'm overextended."

The Lone Voice whispers, "Ministry is not a source of joy; it is a by-product. The source of joy is Jesus Christ. When you are in fellowship with Him, you have it."

* *The FCW thinks*, "When I'm running on empty, I must keep on going, trusting God to make me a blessing anyway."

The Lone Voice whispers, "A vessel that's empty has nothing to offer. Only when your heart is full can joy overflow to others."

* *The FCW thinks*, "Susan has more demands on her time than I, but she is always happy to take on that extra job. I should be like her."

The Lone Voice whispers, "Be careful about comparing yourself with others. What is right for one isn't necessarily right for the other. Each must learn to accept herself: limitations as well as abilities, for God has designed both."

* *The FCW thinks*, "In order to make a favorable impression, I must pretend everything is all right even when it isn't. I must smile when I feel like screaming and reach out to hug when I feel like hiding. And when people ask, 'How are you doing?' I'm expected to answer 'Fine.' To tell how I really feel would be a poor testimony. I don't want to discredit God's grace."

The Lone Voice whispers, "God doesn't need a Christian's hypocrisy to lend credence to His grace. There's a place for an honest expression of how you feel. After all, Jesus wasn't smiling on the cross. He was in agony of soul and let it be known.

"When God promises joy, He is talking about an internal state of peace—something unrelated to circumstances, feelings, or how you express those feelings. Therefore, feel free to weep, cry out, even scream if you want to, and your joy won't be affected at all. It's rooted in the unchangeable character of Christ.

A Divine Perspective

One day as I was preparing a message for a speaking engagement, I turned to the book of Philippians. A key verse leaped out at me. "Rejoice in the Lord always," I read. "I will say it again, Rejoice!" (4:4).

"Now, Lord," I found myself protesting, "You can't mean always. 'Sometimes' I can handle, but not always. You see, we humans are accustomed to rejoicing when things go well. When a loved one comes to the Lord, when a lab report is negative, when there's enough money to pay the bills, when interpersonal relationships are tension free, when the job seems secure, when our elderly parents are managing by themselves, when the programs at church are running smoothly, when at the end of a day every item on our list has been crossed off, then we rejoice.

"But, as You know, things don't always run smoothly down here on Planet Earth. There are times when we're laughed at for our faith, our medical tests reveal malignancies, there's not enough money to meet our obligations, our marriages fall apart, our kids get in with the wrong crowd, we get laid off at work, our elderly parents get sick, there's a major problem at church, and our daily routine overwhelms us. You don't expect us to rejoice then, do You?"

"Yes," the answer came. "I do. But don't confuse joy with happiness. There is a big difference. While happiness is like a boat riding up and down with the waves, joy is more like a treasure chest, settled on the ocean floor. Unaffected by the swirling storms above, it just lies there, becoming more and more precious as time goes by. That's why you can have joy even when you're unhappy. You can actually despise your circumstances and still rejoice in your Lord."

I was intrigued. So I flipped back to the beginning of the book. As I read, I was reminded that Philippians is a prison epistle, written by the apostle Paul while he was still in bonds. No stranger to trials, the apostle, I remembered, had written in his first letter to the Corinthians:

I have been in prison . . . been flogged . . . and been exposed to death again and again. Five times I received from the Jews the forty lashes minus one. . . . Three times I was shipwrecked, I spent a night and a day in the open sea. I have been constantly on the move.

I have been in danger from rivers, in danger from bandits, in danger from my own countrymen, in danger from Gentiles, in danger in the city, in danger in the country, in danger at sea; and in danger from false brothers. I have labored and toiled and have often gone without sleep; I have known hunger and thirst and have often gone without food; I have been cold and naked. Besides everything else, I face daily the pressure of my concern for all the churches. (2 Cor. 11:23–28)

"How can a man who has been through so much write a book on joy?" I asked as I turned my attention back to Philippians. I found my answer in the last chapter. "I have learned," the apostle wrote, "to be content whatever the circumstances" (see 4:11).

The phrase "I have learned" leaped out at me. The apostle Paul had to learn to be joyful, I realized. It must have been a difficult lesson for this giant of the faith, but he did master it. If he could do it, so could I.

So I decided to embark on a detailed study of the process that brought the apostle to victory, identifying as I progressed, the various "prisons" that bind me. What if I'm never released? I wondered. Can I still have joy? Absolutely, I would discover, but there are four concepts to be understood and applied.

The first is *purpose*. The apostle Paul was not bent on living for self or even for others. "For to me, to live is Christ," he said. Then he added, "to die is gain." This is flat-out commitment! I thought. The only comparable statement that came to mind was what Job uttered in the midst of his pain: "Though He slay me, yet will I hope in Him" (Job 13:15).

Then I thought of other reasons for which we humans live and how frustrated we are when we don't reach our goals. For example, we live to get married and it never happens. Or to have children— and it never happens. Or to become famous—and it never happens. Or to gain wealth—and it never happens. Or to lose weight . . . (I couldn't bring myself to say it!).

How easily circumstances can frustrate human purposes, I decided. The only purpose that cannot be frustrated is to live flat-out for Christ. In fact, adverse circumstances actually work for, rather than against, this goal. People watch how Christians handle their trials; thus, trials become opportunities to let our lights shine. This study was getting exciting.

The second concept I concentrated on was Paul's *perspective*. He truly had "the mind of Christ." He was willing to go through the hard places to get to the victory God had promised. In fact, he said, "I want to know Christ and the power of His resurrection and the fellowship of sharing in His sufferings, becoming like Him in His death, and so, somehow, to attain to the resurrection from the dead (Phil. 3:10–11).

Then I read the words: "Your attitude should be the same as that of Christ Jesus" (2:5). Oooh . . . the passage was speaking directly to me. I did want my attitude to be like Christ's. I knew that. But it would take a lot more learning. I had made a start, though, and I really couldn't wait to continue.

Paul's third secret to contentment was proper *priorities* ("I feel like I've been down this road already, Lord," I said. "Go down it again," He replied. So I did.) I was heartened to discover this time I would be evaluating things as opposed to relationships. A refreshing approach, I concluded. Paul's "things" seemed to be divided into three categories: first, things he felt pressured to accumulate; second, things he needed to do; and third, things he wanted to control.

Regarding accumulation, the apostle said, "I consider everything a loss compared to the surpassing greatness of knowing Christ Jesus my Lord" (3:7).

Referring to what he had to do (or thought he had to do), he said, "one thing I do" (v. 13). I was getting convicted.

And concerning things he felt possessive about, he pointed to a Savior who brings "everything under His control" (v. 21). When I got to this Scripture, I wanted to run and hide in shame. But I was compelled to keep on reading.

Last, I noticed Paul's *perseverance.* He talked about "press[ing] on toward the goal" (3:14) and being able to "do everything through Him who gives . . . strength" (4:13). As I read these words, I pictured myself inside a car, chugging along the highways of life. Unlike my friend Katie, I wasn't going to work, to school, nor to church. I was just going.

When I came to a hill, I would put on the gas (I would "press on," so to speak). When I came to a slope, I would tend to coast down. But then I would find myself unprepared for the next hill. Did the apostle Paul mean to "press on" continually? I asked. I concluded he did.

Suddenly, my car's fuel was mentally transformed into joy. I noticed the tank registered full. But unless I stepped on the accelerator, nothing would happen. No joy would flow. When I did press down, joy would be released—enough, I noticed, to maneuver me successfully through any road condition I faced. The responsibility clearly lay with me.

Concepts I had been pondering were starting to make sense now. Christ's determination to endure the pain of the cross was what released the joy that was "set before Him." Because the apostle Paul "pressed on," he eventually learned to be content in any situation. If I could just hang in there, being faithful to my own tasks (whatever the tasks at hand happened to be), God would make me joyful and content. That was His promise. "I can do everything through Him who gives me strength," I recited. The responsibility is mine, but the power is His. Therefore, my focus has to stay on Him. I could hardly wait to get started.

What Can We Do to Change Things?

Respell JOY. The traditional message this acrostic sends is "Put the Lord first, others second, and yourself last," as follows:

J esus
O thers
Y ou

There is indeed some merit in this order. Jesus will come first in a committed Christian's life. And putting others before ourselves indicates a sincere desire to be selfless.

However, there is a problem if our ministry to others is allowed to come between us and our Lord, robbing us of needed refueling time. There is another problem if our personal needs continually end up behind everybody else's. When these two conditions exist, there is no joy for anybody.

When I realized the error this acrostic could teach, I figured I would have to throw out the acronym altogether—something I was hesitant to do because I liked the idea of having a simple formula for living joyfully. Then I conducted a seminar for women in the South. And thanks to some creative women, a new message developed using the same acronym. They spelled JOY as follows:

J esus
O urselves
Y 'all

Thank you, Southern Belles, for showing us that by keeping ourselves close to God, we'll have plenty to offer the world. And our offering will come back to us as joy.

Assess what's making demands on our time and personal resources:

Children	Husband	Job	Self
TV	Pets	Neighbors	Church
Parents	Friends	God	Chores
Ministry	Grooming	Community	Relatives

Ponder:
- Which are taking too much time?
- Which are being neglected?
- Do I feel God is pleased with my priorities?
- What can I change so my priorities are more in line with God's desires?

Schedule a regular devotional time and guard it jealously. Meeting with the Lord is how we get filled up. And returning for fellowship regularly is how we stay filled up. A woman who is joyful has learned to minister from her overflow, not from her reserves. And she knows where the source of that overflow is.

Be honest about how we feel. True joy comes not from plastic smiles and "I'm fine" responses but from freely sharing our pain. Only after our negative feelings have been expressed, can we tap our positive resources. On the way to the cross, Jesus cried, "Take this cup from me"—an honest outburst of frustration. However, He was quick to add, "Yet not my will, but Yours be done" (Luke 22:42). Christ's honesty calls us to be honest too—with Him, with ourselves, and with others—in that order. Then peace, even joy, is free to come.

Confirmation from God's Word

1. Read Ephesians 5:15–6:20 redeeming the time.
2. Notice the joyful admonition in verses 19 and 20.
3. Now notice the interpersonal obligations the apostle Paul addresses and the order in which they come:
    a. J esus: my obligation to the Lord (5:17)
    b. O urselves: my obligation to "me" (5:18–20)
    c. Y 'all: my obligations to others (5:21–6:20)
        1. Husband-wife relationships (5:22–33)
        2. Parent-child relationships (6:1–4)
        3. Work relationships (6:5–10)
        4. Relationships between believers (6:18)
        5. The believers' relationship to the world (6:19–20)
4. What are our obligations in each of these relationships? What specific joys will each act of obedience bring?
5. Do you see any significance to the fact that while addressing interpersonal obligations, Paul inserts a paragraph on fortifying ourselves, on putting on the "armor of God" (6:10–17)?

When a woman is dressed well, she usually feels good. Others notice her self-assurance and compliment her. The result is joy—all around.

Do you notice any similarities between being dressed well physically and being dressed well spiritually? Explain.

Each of us tends to be,
not a single self,
but a whole committee of selves.
There is the civic self, the parental self,
the financial self, the religious self, the society self,
the professional self, the literary self . . .
—Thomas Kelly, A Testament of Devotion

4

Reach Out Farther!

"Truly I say to you, to the extent that you did it to one of these
brothers of Mine, even the least of them, you did it to Me."
Matthew 25:40, NASB

"**H**ey, look at this one!" Jeff called to Greg as he held up a shiny stone.

Greg ran along the bank of the pond until he reached his twin brother. Then he took the rock Jeff was displaying, turned it over, and announced, "I've got a better one. Watch."

With all the strength an eleven-year-old can muster, Greg swung his arm back from his shoulder and heaved his missile as far as he could. It sailed toward the center of the pond.

Plop! It sank immediately. As it did, a circle of water shot upward, then slid into a ridge that moved rapidly outward. Concentric ripples formed, first one, then another, then another, but none matched the impact of the original burst.

I stood there on the bank, fascinated. As the original ripple moved in my direction, I noticed its energy was being dissipated. Soon the only activity in the pond was on the periphery. The point of impact was calm.

"Who said, 'The farther the outreach, the better?'" I asked myself.

"Plenty of people," a voice inside responded.

Listen to the Many Voices

(Note: The words *ministry, service,* and *outreach* are used interchangeably to signify whatever the FCW is involved in to advance the kingdom of God.)

    * "One-to-one is fine for starters, but your aim should be the multitudes."

    * "The measuring stick of an effective ministry is how far and wide it extends."

    * "Go into full-time Christian service. God deserves your all."

    * "To make your life count, prepare for the foreign mission field."

    * "Whatever you're doing now should not be considered an end in itself. God always has more for you."

All voices in unison: "Bigger is better. Seek ways to expand."

Our response: "I've heard about the stressed-out woman, who after receiving a request from the Red Cross, screamed, 'And now they want my blood!'? Well, it couldn't be said any better. That's exactly how I feel. What can I do?"

A Lone Voice: " Why don't you tune out the other voices and tune in only to Mine? I will give you rest."

Accentuating the Positive

The mountain air was crisp that autumn day in New Hampshire, providing a perfect environment for our interdenominational retreat. At breakfast a pastor's wife had asked if we could have an informal sharing time between scheduled sessions—reserved exclusively for pastors' wives. I readily agreed. What an opportunity to gain insight—from women who were really stressed out in ministry!

The room chosen for the meeting was bare and unheated, but by the time I got there, folding chairs formed a circle and a fire was crackling in the fireplace. How good it felt to warm up!

The women arrived one by one until our group numbered an even dozen. "Why don't we introduce ourselves and tell something about our various ministries?" I ventured.

The sharing began. Almost immediately so did the tears. Ginny had recently lost a daughter to cancer and was blaming herself for spending too much time at the hospital and not enough with her Bible class. Maryleigh said her family life was being disrupted by increasing numbers of women coming for counseling. And Jean was trying to care for her husband's ailing mother—along with everything else a pastor's wife is supposed to do. But all these women shared a common problem: they were being pressured to increase, not decrease, their level of involvement.

We hugged, shared words of comfort, even advice, then settled down to do some serious thinking. "Tell me," I began, "is there anything positive about the pressure to expand and enlarge a ministry?"

"I can think of something," Jean said. "Christ gave His disciples a blueprint for spreading the gospel. It was 'first in Jerusalem, then in Judea, then in Samaria, and then to the uttermost part of the earth.' That's a mandate for expansion if I ever heard one."

"What about actively promoting growth?" I asked. "Can anybody think of a reason why a group should make an effort to grow in numbers?"

"Sure," Ginny volunteered. "A ministry that is not growing will eventually die. That's what's happening to my home Bible study. The women are so comfortable with each other they get threatened at the thought of inviting others to join them. We're becoming stagnant."

"What Christians don't realize," Jean philosophized, "—and I'm as guilty as anyone else—is that when a ministry begins, it's meant to go somewhere, to branch out, to expand."

"And to actively strive to do so?" I asked.

"Why not?" Jean countered. "It's an effort in the right direction."

"So there is something positive about the pressures Christian 'movers and shakers' are putting on the rest of us. Right?"

Several women nodded, but their faces showed concern. Something important had been left unsaid.

Maryleigh rescued us. "In the push to meet the needs of the whole world," she said, "ministries can lose their focus and leaders can become fractured. How can we keep this from happening?"

The next section is a compilation of what these pastors' wives came up with that day. They began by examining the pressure—the messages they are hearing; then, Bibles in hand, they sought to ferret out the errors.

Overstatement and Truth

* *The FCW thinks,* "Small ministries are insignificant."

The Lone Voice whispers, "Small ministries are very significant, sometimes the most significant of all. In the long run, Jesus accomplished more with the Twelve than with the multitudes. Likewise, you may do more for the Kingdom through offering one cup of cold water in the name of the Lord than trying to dump an entire ocean on rocky soil."

* *The FCW thinks*, "The farther you travel with the gospel, the more obedient you are. I should become a foreign missionary."

The Lone Voice whispers, "God's will has less to do with geography and more with being in the appointed place at the appointed time. Are you where God wants you now? That's the question."

* *The FCW thinks*, "God wants people who are totally committed, so I should consider full-time Christian service."

The Lone Voice whispers, "In Christian service all are totally committed. There is no part-time ministry. And there is no distinction between the salaried and volunteers, clergy and laity, foreign missionaries and those who share their faith at home. All serve fully. They can't help it, for their faith is not a garment they put on when doing something 'Christian.' It's their skin."

* *The FCW thinks*, "To prepare for greater outreach, I should take some courses. I'll have to give up my teaching, witnessing, and counseling to do this. But I need training."

The Lone Voice whispers, "It doesn't make sense to give up successful ministries to train for what you hope will be more successful ones—unless, of course, God tells you to. How-to knowledge is good, but let's remember Jesus chose uneducated fishermen, as well as scholars, to reach the world with His love. What counts is not how much you're learning but how effectively you're using what you already know.

"Of course there will be some who will say, 'You can't serve until you're ready.' But who is ever ready? There will always be questions you cannot answer, personalities you cannot handle, and situations you cannot address. Don't let these hurdles stop you. Get out there and do what needs to be done—and learn how in the process. Otherwise, you'll miss out on many blessings."

* *The FCW thinks*, "*More* seems to be Christianity's pet motivational word: do more; reach more; be more. Always strive to expand."

The Lone Voice whispers, "Sometimes less is more. Think of the widow's mite, the one kind act, the single word of encouragement. Small ministries do count, often more than large, impressive ones. Just be faithful."

A Divine Perspective

One evening as I was watching the national news on TV, I learned that Mother Teresa of Calcutta was ill. In 1979 I was reminded, she had received the Nobel Peace Prize for serving her fellowman. What a ministry God has entrusted to her, I thought.

It began on a street in India when she picked up one dying person. Today her Missionaries of Charity are caring for the destitute and dying in fifty-two countries around the world.

As graphic scenes of her compassionate outreach flashed on the screen, I became more taken than ever with this humble woman's dedication. "I have heard Christians question her theology," I mused. "But I have never heard anybody criticize her service."

Then I asked myself, "Would she have received the Nobel Peace Prize if her ministry had stayed small?"

Probably not, I surmised.

But is that the issue? Isn't this the issue: Is Mother Teresa doing what God wants Mother Teresa to do where God wants Mother Teresa to do it at this moment in Mother Teresa's life?

Next I evaluated my own ministry. Not very impressive compared to Mother Teresa's. So for encouragement I tuned to the parable of the talents in Matthew 25 (NASB). As I read, I was introduced again to the three servants to whom the master entrusted money. One servant took his talent and buried it. He was rebuked when his master returned for an accounting.

The other two, though entrusted with unequal amounts, invested their gifts wisely; and in both cases their investments multiplied. Consequently, to both of them the master said, "You have been faithful with a few things; I will put you in charge of many things" (v. 21).

"Thank You, Lord!" I exclaimed as the light dawned. "The expansion or non-expansion of my ministry is Your responsibility. My responsibility is faithfulness. Is Peg Rankin doing what You want Peg Rankin to do, where You want Peg Rankin to do it at this moment in Peg Rankin's life? If I minister to thousands, fine. If I minister to hundreds, that's fine too. And if I give just one cup of water to only one lone soul, that too is significant. Now help me live this truth."

I went to my bookshelf and pulled down Mother Teresa's book, *Words to Love By*. As I reread it, I discovered her secret: faithfulness to the seemingly insignificant, attention to the "one":

I never look at the masses as my responsibility. I look at the individual. I can love only one person at a time. I can feed only one person at a time. Just one, one, one . . .

As Jesus said, "Whatever you do to the least of my brethren, you do to me." So you begin . . . I begin. I picked up one person—maybe if I didn't pick up that one person I wouldn't have picked up 42,000. The whole work is only a drop in the ocean. But if I didn't put the drop in, the ocean would be one drop less.

Same thing for you, same thing in your family, same thing in the church where you go; just begin . . . one, one, one.[3]

With these words entrenched in my mind, I went to church for a regular Sunday morning worship service. Amazingly, the pastor was speaking on serving others. He closed his message with a paraphrase from the Russian fiction writer Leo Tolstoy. "There are three questions people ask," the pastor said, "when they are seeking to make their lives significant:

1. Who is the most important person?
2. What is the most important thing?
3. What is the most important time to do it?

The correct answers, however, may not be what significance-seekers are expecting. For the most important person is the person you are with, the most important thing is what needs to be done, and the most important time to do it is now."

I left the church bursting with blessing.

What Can We Do to Change Things?

Commit this moment and this activity to God. "Right now, Lord, I wish I were somewhere else doing something different. But I am where I am, doing what I'm doing by Your grace. May I work at my task wholeheartedly, holding nothing back, for You are watching me and I want You to be pleased" (see Eph. 6:7).

Dr. Martin Luther King, Jr. understood this concept of giving our all:

Whatever your life's work is, do it well. A man should do his job so well that the living, the dead and the unborn could do it no better.

If it falls your lot to be a street sweeper, sweep streets like Michelangelo painted pictures, like Shakespeare wrote poetry, like Beethoven composed music; sweep streets so well that all the hosts of heaven and earth will have to pause and say, "Here lived a great street sweeper, who swept his job well." [4]

Approach each activity as a Christian opportunity. Whether we're involved in the sacred or the secular, in the home or outside the home, we have one Boss, the Lord Jesus Christ, and it is Him we are serving (see Col. 3:23). Therefore, it is our job to make our Boss "look good" (as they say in the parlance of business).

I'm not quite sure when the role of parent-teaching-child gets reversed, but when it happens it is awesome to behold. We were seated at our son Dirk's kitchen table in his home in suburban Baltimore, talking about his busy life. He was struggling with trying to be a good husband, father, government employee, church deacon, trumpeter in the church orchestra, member of a small group Bible study, and candidate for his Master's degree at Johns Hopkins University. It wasn't easy. He was a Fractured Christian Male, strung out about as far as he could go.

"Of all these commendable activities," I asked as the conversation progressed, "which do you feel offers you the greatest opportunity to serve your Lord?"

He didn't hesitate. "My work with the National Security Agency," he replied.

I almost fell off my evangelical seat. "He's backslidden," I lamented. "He's got his priorities all wrong. Why didn't he say his work at church? Or at home with the kids? Why at the government?"

So I asked him (notice the tact here), "Why didn't you say your church work—or your influence at home? Why your government job?"

"Because that's where my light shines the brightest, Mom," he replied.

I was stunned. Then I realized he was right. At church there were lots of lights. Even at home there was Laurie's light. But in his government office, he was it. That was where the Lord had placed him to do the Lord's work. And he wanted to make His Lord "look good."

As I shimmied back to the center of my evangelical seat, I noticed it was stronger now. "Thank you, Dirk," I said. "And thank

You, Lord," I added. "Now help me apply this truth to my own life."

Take advantage of ministry helps without overloading the schedule. There are books, tapes, and courses filled with tips on how to serve others more effectively. While we are learning how to do it, though, we may want to take a look around. In our class on witnessing, is there someone who needs a witness? In our course on counseling, is there a classmate needing counsel? It's possible to get so involved in planning what we're going to do *when*, we miss the need that's here *now*.

Be faithful stewards over the ministries God has given and leave the results to Him. There is a divinely approved middle ground between charging ahead of God and lagging behind, and it is not always easy to discern. To determine exactly what this middle ground implies, I decided to elicit help from a class of adults my husband and I were teaching.

"Considering all the road signs and traffic signals you can think of," I ventured, "which best typifies the Christian life?"

The class thought for a moment. Then someone shouted, "Go!"

I smiled, then said, "I appreciate why you said that, for Christians are expected to be active. However, too many of us are pressing on the accelerator so hard, God is left standing in the exhaust fumes. Think again."

"Stop!" someone else yelled. Again I smiled. "Considering the first answer I can see why you chose that one," I commented. "And indeed, there are times to be still and know, simply, that He is God. But there are too many Christians in this camp too—at the stop sign, stuck. In fact, some have shifted into 'Park.' Think again."

John raised his hand. A father of five daughters and a Christian who really wants his life to count, John made his contribution quietly. "Yield," he said.

"You've got it, John!" I affirmed. "Neither accelerating into passing gear nor content to remain locked in 'Park,' these Christians have already shifted out of neutral and are poised with their eyes on the rear-view mirror, ready. The minute their Lord appears, they move out, positioning themselves behind Him as He advances. As fast as He goes, they go, no faster. As far as He goes, they go, no farther. They are comfortable in the flow of His Spirit. It's the only way to move forward in faith."

Later on, John would write to Lee and me, sharing what that

particular class had meant to him. "Each time I stop at a Yield sign while driving," he penned, "I'm reminded of you. Have you noticed the shape of a yield sign? It is a triangle (Trinity) with a red border (the blood of Christ shed for you and me) and a pure white center imprinted with one word: Yield. How generous of our Lord to leave road signs with the only direction to heaven."

Focus rather than fragmentize. If we're doing too much, let's eliminate. If we're too spread out, let's pull back. If our efforts are being dissipated, let's concentrate them. A large stone hurled at a particular spot in a pond will make a much greater impact than a lot of pebbles thrown at random, and the ripples won't confuse each other with their overlap.

Confirmation from God's Word

1. Read John 13:1–17 about Jesus washing the disciples' feet.
2. Assume the role of a journalist, reporting an incident:
   - When does Jesus serve (why then)?
   - Where does He serve (why there)?
   - What type of service does He render (why this)?
   - How many does He serve?
   - Does He serve any "difficult" people?
   - For what purpose does He serve (temporarily, ultimately)?
3. Ponder:
   - What must it feel like to serve someone you know is going to betray you (see v. 2)?
   - If the towel Jesus is using is draped over His belt (see vv. 4–5), then where does the dirt end up? Am I willing to take on somebody else's "dirt"?
   - What's the best way to handle someone who doesn't want to be served (see v. 8)?
   - How about someone who wants you to do more for him than you originally intended (see v. 9)?
   - Are any of the disciples in a position to repay the kindness Jesus is rendering? Does it matter?
   - Will the disciples' feet get dirty again?
4. Jesus said, "I have given you an example that you should do as I have done to you" (v. 15). What can the FCW learn from Christ's example?

Part Two

The Fracturing
that Results

In play you can abandon yourself.
You can immerse yourself
without restraint, you can pierce
life's complexities and confusions.
You can become whole again without even trying.
—Tim Hansel[5]

5

Help! I'm Coming Apart!

Create in me a pure heart, O God, and renew a steadfast spirit
within me. Restore to me the joy of your salvation
and grant me a willing spirit, to sustain me.
Psalm 51:10,12

Methodically, I opened the box that contained the brown sugar I needed for my candied sweet potato recipe. Since the sugar was new, I had to slit its plastic wrapper. After measuring out the correct amount, I folded the plastic and searched for a rubber band to secure it.

In a drawer of kitchen utensils I spotted one. It looked frayed from use. "Can I get one more stretch out of it?" I wondered. Carefully, I pulled the ends of the band to cover the length of the rectangle. Snap!

"I was afraid of that," I said to myself. "I guess I stretched it once too often." I tried hard not to think about what that broken rubber band was saying to me. But I was unsuccessful. Its message was coming from everywhere: loud, clear, and very, very convicting.

Listen to the Many Voices

* "Be serious. There is little time for laughter when the needs of the world are so great."

* "Get yourself organized and keep a full schedule. Christian

women should be 'super women,' able to do more than others."

* "Set goals for your life and push yourself to achieve them. When you stand before God in judgment, you want to be able to say, 'I made my life count, Lord.'"

* "Vacations are for those whose obligations have been completed. Really dedicated people take little time off."

* "Burning out for God? Rejoice! There's a reward in heaven for those who are 'martyred' for their faith."

All voices in unison: "Don't say you don't have time to take on added responsibilities. People find time for what is important to them."

Our response: "How long can I keep up this pace? Something's got to give."

A Lone Voice: "Don't let it be your spirituality. Listen to Me—and only to Me. My voice will be a relaxing influence when you feel ready to break."

Accentuating the Positive

Shirl, the leader of our church women's group, was sitting across the table at our spring luncheon. I was impressed with how effectively she had run our program this year. Since she had five kids and a husband to care for, I wondered how she found time for church work. I decided to ask her.

"I don't have a choice," she told me. "I came into the Christian faith expecting to serve," she explained. "When I found a need, I pitched in. I've been pitching in ever since. I love being part of something eternal. It beats cleaning house and washing dishes—although they're important, too."

I identified with her remarks. "But how do you find time for all you do?"

"People make time for what's important to them," Shirl stated while looking in her purse. "Everybody has twenty-four hours in a day. You either waste it or invest it." She ran some lipstick over her lips and then pressed them together. "I want to invest it."

Feeling a tinge of guilt, I blurted, "You must be a very organized person."

"'Structured' is what my husband calls me," she smiled.

"Mind sharing your secret?" I asked.

"I don't know if it's a secret," Shirl answered, "but I do set goals—goals for each day, each week, each month, and for the year. Of course, with a family as big as ours, you have to be flexible. There are always things to sidetrack you. Plus an occasional emergency," she added.

When she mentioned the word *emergency*, I thought, "Isn't it amazing how the busiest among us get called upon to do that extra job—that 'emergency'? And they always get it done."

"Are your goals specific?" I asked, eager to learn more.

"They have to be," Shirl explained. "If you don't define a bullseye, you may not even hit the target."

I smiled. "I'm going to start calling you Super Woman."

Shirl laughed. "Every woman is a super woman when she has the Holy Spirit."

"For sure," I admitted soberly. "But, tell me, do you ever play?"

"Certainly," Shirl said, "but work comes first. I find if I play first, I don't always have time for everything that's important. But if I work first, I not only get my jobs done, I enjoy my recreation more. Besides, I don't want to be caught 'playing' when the Lord returns. There's a big world to reach and limited time to do it in."

"I can't argue with that. But what if you burn out?" I asked.

"Nobody wants to burn out," Shirl admitted, "but if it does happen, it can end up positively. I just saw a TV special that gave me new insight on burn-out."

"Was it the documentary about the fire in Yellowstone National Park in 1988?" I questioned, my creative juices flowing.

"Yes," Shirl enthused. "The experts thought the park was finished as a major tourist attraction. But they ruled out the power of God, didn't they?"

"They sure did. I loved that special. Do you remember how the narrator said a year after the fire there was hardly any evidence of the devastation?"

"Yes, new shoots of grass were dotting the blackened landscape. Pine cones, forced open by the heat, were releasing the makings of a new forest. And plants that were previously inedible became delicious in the nitrogen-enriched soil. Amazing! But the climax came with that panoramic shot of wild flowers that bloom only after a fire. Remember?"

"I sure do," I recalled enthusiastically. "They have made Yellowstone more beautiful than ever!"

"I believe the same thing can happen after emotional burn-out," Shirl continued. "It can result in a whole new beginning. I watched this happen to my brother.

"He was the pastor of a growing congregation. The demands on his time were so overwhelming that one day he just burned out. In his case I believe God is the One who set the fire because my brother had lots of debris in his life. But now that the junk is gone and he's had time to recover, he's talking about starting a new ministry, perhaps counseling people with burn-out."

Shirl chuckled. But she was so full of insight, I hardly noticed. I decided to ask her to help me study the time pressures of women who are approaching burn-out but don't want to go through the process.

"Who does?" she queried. But she agreed to help. So together we studied the messages fractured Christian women are hearing.

Overstatement and Truth

* *The FCW thinks*, "I've got to keep taking on more, for I can never do enough for God."

The Lone Voice whispers, "Why do you picture God standing over you with a pen and performance sheet in hand? He is your loving heavenly Father, providing everything you need to enjoy life richly and fully."

* *The FCW thinks*, "In terms of time, energy, and capabilities, there should be no limit to what a Christian can do."

The Lone Voice whispers, "Christian or not, you are human. And humans get tired, discouraged, and depleted. They need breaks. And they need them regularly. Recognize the wisdom in recreation and in the God who lovingly provides it."

* *The FCW thinks*, "If people are saying something is important for me to do, then it is, in fact, important for me to do."

The Lone Voice whispers, "You are allowing others to impose their values on you, when it would be better to come to your own conclusions in the light of God's Word."

* *The FCW thinks*, "I must stick to my schedule. To do less is to betray myself."

The Lone Voice whispers, "When a Christian woman becomes a slave to her own organizational skills, she robs herself of many blessings: the joy of the unexpected, the surprise of the unplanned, and the thrill of living in wide-eyed anticipation of how God might move. In your daily living make sure you don't miss life."

* *The FCW thinks*, "If I don't achieve my goals, I am a failure."

The Lone Voice whispers, "You're ruling out God's power. God can take what you consider failure and turn it into success. But you must let Him."

* *The FCW thinks*, "I get annoyed with interruptions. They steal time from more important things."

"*The Lone Voice whispers*, "Interruptions become divine appointments when God takes control. Think positively."

* *The FCW thinks*, "I wish I could take time to laugh. But life is much too serious."

The Lone Voice whispers, "You *must* take time to laugh. Seeing humor in everyday situations will serve to relax you, keeping you from breaking when you're being stretched too far."

* *The FCW thinks*, "My obligations will eventually let up. Then I can take a vacation without feeling guilty."

The Lone Voice whispers, "Obligations never let up. When one responsibility is discharged, there is always another to take its place. It will be so even when you have departed this planet. Then what will happen to your obligations? Yet life will still go on.

"So take a break whenever you can afford to—and even when you think you can't. And don't feel guilty. God ordained rest. He even modeled it when He observed the first Sabbath. Do the same, as the fourth commandment teaches. 'Come apart once a week for the purpose of honoring God. And you will benefit not only spiritually but physically as well.'"

* *The FCW thinks*, "Since God desires excellence, my driven feeling must be coming from Him."

The Lone Voice whispers, "Don't blame God for your fractured lifestyle. You have made a choice. You have chosen to be driven—and not by your heavenly Father. It is the system that is propelling you. But you are allowing it to happen. You've accepted your overloaded schedule as normal. Why? Because to question it would require you to do something about it—to become a self-starter, so to speak. And what Christian woman wants to self-start when she can be driven with much less effort? It's a subtle trap, isn't it? But a trap not without release."

* **The FCW thinks**, "It's better not to fight the system. If I burn out, so be it."

The Lone Voice whispers, "Burn-out can be beneficial, but only when it comes from God. Otherwise, it can be disastrous. So take precautions to prevent it. Plan periods of non-productivity. Be on the watch during dry times. And when you see a spark that looks dangerous, act quickly. Be as alert to your spiritual condition as God is."

A Divine Perspective

It was going to be tight. I knew that. I was due to speak at a Lutheran Lenten service in Toledo in two hours, and I had been told to allow an hour and a half for the drive. Because we had recently moved to the Midwest and the surroundings were strange, my husband Lee had consented to chauffeur me. But he wasn't even home from work yet. What to do?

Before I could answer my own question, Lee burst through the door. I was ready. I called the kids, slid food onto our plates, and Lee said grace on the way to his seat. Then we bolted down our dinner, Lee picked up the sitter, and after a few instructions we kissed the kids good-bye. As Lee and I flew out the door, I grabbed my new white coat.

We hadn't gotten more than a few blocks when the car stopped running. It didn't cough, sputter, writhe, or shudder. It just died.

As we were trying to figure out what to do, a truck pulled up beside us.

"What seems to be the problem?" the driver asked, as he rolled down the window.

We were so new to the area we had made very few friends, but that driver—Larry—was one of them. Having worked all day with machines, he was covered with grime, but to me he looked like an angel.

Lee explained the situation as best he could, emphasizing the time constraint. Then we mentioned that we had another car, but it was back in our garage.

"Get in," Larry motioned. We did, me squeezing in the middle in my new white coat.

Larry dropped off Lee at a service station, then turned his

truck in the direction of our subdivision. "I'm never going to make it," I moaned as I slid to the right.

Larry stepped on the gas.

Suddenly from out of nowhere appeared a police car, lights flashing. Larry pulled over.

When the representative of the law came within hearing range, Larry blurted, "Officer, I've got to explain. This woman is not my wife. I just picked her up."

I tried to appear invisible.

Larry continued, "Her car just broke down. I'm rushing her home to get her other one. She's due to speak in Toledo at 7:30. Could I come back and pay the fine?"

I could tell the officer was studying Larry, greasy overalls and all. Then he looked at me in my new white coat. That clinched it. The story must be true. With a wave of his hand he dismissed us. "Get going, buddy," he said. We did.

Once behind the wheel of my car, I waved good-bye to my benefactor and peeled out of the driveway before the kids had a chance to realize Mommy had returned.

Cautiously, I turned onto the main drag. Suddenly there were gas stations everywhere. I thought only rabbits multiplied that quickly. I had been too upset earlier to notice where Larry had dropped off Lee, so I pulled into the first station I came to. No husband. Then into another. Still no familiar face.

Then I caught sight of a man in a business suit a short distance down the road. He was waving wildly.

I pulled over and slid to the passenger side. Lee got into the driver's seat. We were off, both of us breathing easier.

We had gone only a few miles, however, when Lee noticed the fuel gauge was approaching empty. "We've got to stop for gas," he announced. I groaned.

"We'd better phone the church and say we're going to be late," I suggested.

"I'll do it," Lee volunteered.

As I sat there, watching the attendant shake a few more drops into the tank, I could feel my frustration rising to my cheeks (it was already doing a job on my heart). I tried to calm myself.

"They have decided to begin the service without you," Lee informed me when he returned. "Your part comes after the offering. We should make it."

"I hope so," I ventured. Then it occurred to me that Lutherans run everything according to a certain order of worship. Why couldn't this have happened when I was scheduled with some Pentecostal group, where ritual is unheard of and the only rule they know is to "hang loose and let go"?

Lee paid the attendant, started the car, and merged into traffic. When we reached the Toledo area, we tried to follow our instructions precisely. It was hard to read the street signs in the dwindling light. However, we arrived at what we thought was the correct church. I leaped out only to discover the sign in front said Methodist.

Back in the car, we proceeded, checking every steeple along the way. By this time my heart was out of control. Frantic? Frazzled? Fractured? Fragmented? All these words together could not describe the woman seated next to my husband.

Finally we found it: the Lutheran church! A "sentry" was posted at the door. "You're here," she greeted me. "The ushers are taking the offering."

"Do I have time to go to the bathroom?" I queried. "Hmm, . . . let me rephrase that. I have to go to the bathroom. Where is it?"

The sentry ushered me downstairs and pointed out the ladies' room. As I entered, she stayed outside, guarding the door.

Inside were several stalls, each with wooden doors that came within inches of the floor. I chose the closest, stepped inside, and slid the bolt.

When it was time to leave, I grabbed the bolt—the same bolt that had just slid easily. It refused to budge. I tried again. Not even a fraction of an inch! I reached to the top of the door and tried to rock it free. Seconds were ticking away.

"Maybe I can think skinny and slither underneath," I thought, scrutinizing the twelve-inch allowance. Then I remembered I was wearing a wig. Wigs were popular back then, and mine gave me that "professionally done" look when the real me underneath was anything but. The wig's last appointment at the beauty parlor had produced an overly teased bouffant.

"The wig and I together will never make it," I concluded. Then the absurdity of the situation struck me. Here I was only a few feet from my destination and unable to get there because I was locked in the bathroom!

"Help!" I shouted. "I can't get out of here."

The sentry appeared. "I'll rock from my side and you rock from yours," she suggested. We did. And after several attempts, the door gave way. I was free.

I glanced in the mirror, adjusted my wig, and bounded upstairs, leaving the sentry behind. My route brought me to the back of the sanctuary.

"We welcome to our service this evening Mrs. Peg Rankin," the announcer said, "who will bring us our Lenten message."

Feeling like O. J. Simpson who had just sprinted through the airport to catch a plane but not wanting to look the way I felt, I walked sedately to the front. Although my appearance may have fooled my audience, it didn't fool me. My mind was racing, my heart felt as if it was going to beat itself right out of my chest, and my stomach was processing food at the highest setting.

Once at the podium, I adjusted the mike and scrambled to find the right spot in my notebook. How had I planned to start?

"I must have emptied my brain when I emptied my bladder," I thought. Meanwhile, my heart's frantic beat was beginning to concern me. So was my churning stomach!

I paused. A voice! A still, small voice was struggling to be heard. "Whoa," it whispered. "Slow down."

"Okay," I agreed. "I hear You."

"Now, step back and take a good look at yourself."

I did. "Ridiculous," I assessed. "Absurd."

"Now look at the faces of those you have come to minister to."

"Ridiculous again. Doubly absurd."

"They need release," the voice said. "So do you. So why don't you share what just happened?"

"The whole story?" I asked.

"The whole story," was the reply.

So I did. And that evening in Toledo a very staid Lutheran church broke out in laughter. Good, clean, refreshing laughter. The kind that revives the soul.

As we laughed, our tension began to dissipate. You could almost see the gleeful endorphins racing through our systems. Soon there were smiles everywhere and a few perked-up shoulders as well. The amazing thing is it took God only a few minutes to accomplish this remarkable change. And He did it through humor.

"A cheerful heart is good medicine," He says (see Prov. 17:22). How true! Our laughter had cured our stress. But it had done much more. It had opened our souls to God's truth in a way nothing else could. Without realizing it, we had seen ourselves as God sees us. And because of that, we then could see Him as He wants us to.

As I began my message and we rehearsed the events of Passion Week, we were there—right beside our Savior. We were in the crowd that followed Him up Calvary's hill. We watched as He was nailed to the tree. We winced at the sound of the hammer reverberating down the valley and as He looked down at us from His painful ledge, we gazed back—into eyes of love. One by one we approached the cross and laid at its feet our burdens. And then, in silence, we watched the Savior pay the price for their removal. "Dying for our sins," Christians call it dying for all those times we have fallen short of what God wants us to be. Suddenly it hit us: because Christ had taken our burdens, we could now be free. Because He had suffered in agony, we could now burst into laughter—pure, revitalizing, holy laughter. We just did. And we will again. In fact, we must, for laughter is God's antidote for tension. Laughter is God's doorway to the soul.

What Can We Do to Change Things?

Take on as much as possible, but no more. Most people function best when working at capacity. I do. But we all break down when required to give too much. Most of us know our limits. The question is whether we will honor them by determining when to say yes and when to say no.

Plan, organize, and schedule, but not without flexibility or divine sanction. God often rewrites daily planners. When He does so, He's saying, "This is what I want you to do today."

Once we submit to His control, we're free to approach each day with a positive attitude: "Well, Lord, here it is: another twenty-four hours to be used up as You see fit. I've arranged my schedule to please You. But if You want to rearrange it, that's fine. Just don't let me waste my interruptions or disregard the significance of the changes You make. Rather, let me seize each challenge as Your opportunity."

After commitment comes implementation, which is always the hard part. Let's say the phone rings. We pick it up. As we do, we pray, "Lord, I need wisdom, love, and tact. Could You please give it now—and in abundance?"

A knock comes at the door. We open it. As we give the greeting, we're asking, "Lord, give me Your grace in manner and speech."

There is an unexpected, tense summons to the hospital. We go. On the way we admit, "I don't know what I'm going to see when I get there, Lord, or how I'm going to react. Just make me Your representative, please, and make me a good one." This is overcoming stress God's way.

Set personal goals but make a generous allowance for failure. The big question on Judgment Day will probably not be, "Did you accomplish everything you set out to do on May 22, 1994?" Rather, it will be, "Did you live that day for God?" The Lord wants our hearts more than our efforts, our lives more than our service. We don't have to make quotas, meet deadlines, or accomplish goals. In fact, we can fail—and fail miserably—and still be loved and used for God's purposes. Isn't that a freeing concept?

Schedule personal rest periods. Periodic breaks from routine are necessary. They are "coming apart" times, designed to keep us from—well—coming apart. They include yearly vacations, weekly sabbaths, and moments each day when we create sanctuaries. Kids may be tearing through our house, machines humming at the plant, or traffic whizzing all around, but we are alone, being refreshed. The thing is, though, these breaks may not happen if they are not planned. So we have to "pencil them in."

Someone said, "A vacation is what you take when you can no longer take what you are taking." I think it is better to say, "A vacation is what you take before you get to the place where you can no longer take what you are taking."

Depending on how long a break we can snatch, we may choose to talk with God, meditate on Scripture, listen to music, read a funny book, brush our hair, leaf through a magazine, do our nails, touch our toes, laugh with a friend, or do absolutely nothing— which, we have to remind ourselves, is not a sin. The activity is less important than the time apart. By shifting into neutral for a while, we're revving up for when the light turns green. Then we'll be better workers, better wives, better friends, better mothers, better citizens, and better Christians. We will have been renewed.

Have a good laugh. Sometimes this takes a conscious effort, but, oh, is it worth it! To laugh alone, to laugh with a friend, to laugh as a group—what joy this brings to the soul.

Unfortunately, we have pictured our Savior as the suffering sin-bearer for so long, it has become difficult to picture Him laughing. And yet He must have laughed. When He took into His lap those bubbly children, how did His joy express itself? When He mingled with the happy guests at the wedding of Cana, did He enter into their fun? In the relaxed atmosphere of the home of Mary, Martha, and Lazarus, did laughter occasionally ring from the walls? We'll never know for certain, but it would be strange indeed if Christ did not laugh.

Laughter relieves tension, breaks down barriers, and sends endorphins racing through our systems. No wonder God calls it medicine. No wonder God encourages us to do it.

Confirmation from God's Word

1. Read Hebrews 4:1–11 describing the believer's rest. This is a toughie, but the rewards for digging in are worth the effort.

2. Note: Some commentators feel the writer is talking about three different kinds of rest, and none physical. They all refer to a "ceasing of spiritual activity" with reference to time:

    a. Past rest (v. 3) comes when we realize we no longer have to "work" to achieve salvation. Christ accomplished it; we receive it. Therefore, if we're believers, we already have this rest.

    b. Future rest (v. 9) awaits us in heaven. It is promised to all who trust God. So there need be no unrest concerning our future. It is secure.

    c. Present rest (v. 1) is the elusive one. It requires giving up working for God and instead, letting Him work through us. The key concept here is yielding—giving control to the Spirit and staying out of the way.

3. Would you say most Christian women are falling short of their "present rest"? Why? What are some of the ways we interfere with the Spirit's work? What does lack of faith have to do with unrest (see v. 2)? How about "disobedience" (see vv. 6 and 11)?

4. What is the importance of "today" as it relates to our rest or unrest (see v. 7)?

5. What messages does God's "Sabbath-rest" (His rest from the work of creation) send to fractured women (see v. 9)?

6. Make a list of your weekly activities. Now go down the list, item by item, asking yourself, "Do I experience a sense of peace when I'm involved in this activity? Which activities cause me to feel unsettled? Do you see any correlation between God-directed activities and present rest? How about between self-or-others-imposed activities and present unrest?

7. Do you detect any lack of faith with regard to any of your activities? How about disobedience?

8. Does entering God's present rest involve "effort" (see v. 10–11)? If so, what kind of effort?

9. What physical benefits come from spiritual rest?

10. Are you looking forward to heaven? Why?

Who I am, then, is Christ's.
What that means,
I am still discovering.
What that costs, I shiver to contemplate.
—Elizabeth Cody Newenhuyse[6]

6

My Living Sacrifice Is Dying!

For I delight in loyalty rather than sacrifice
and in the knowledge of God rather than burnt offerings.
Hosea 6:6, NASB

The pastor began his sermon with an illustration: "Picture a flock of sheep grazing peacefully beside a quiet stream. The shepherd is walking through the flock, observing the lambs.

"'I need one without a flaw,' he judges, spying a ram about a year old.

"Quickly he separates the unsuspecting animal from the rest. Then he puts the young ram in a pen by itself, where it will remain for three days.

"Each day the shepherd comes to scrutinize the lamb. When he is satisfied the lamb is without blemish, he picks it up, presses it to his heart, and carries it to the place where sacrifices are made to the one true God.

"Tenderly, the shepherd lays the lamb upon the altar, tying its legs to the horns at each corner. Then he takes from his belt a sharp knife, and with one deft slice, slits the lamb's throat, letting the blood flow."

In my pew I winced. "That poor lamb!"

"The lamb had to die," the pastor continued. "Without the shedding of blood, there is no forgiveness" (Heb. 9:22). Its death foreshadowed Christ's death on the cross, where He made atonement for our sins."

I knew that. I had heard it many times. But this time my mind was racing from the Old Testament to the New, where God requires me to become a sacrifice—a living one at that (see Rom. 12:1)!

"At least when the lamb made its sacrifice, it was over," I reasoned. "After that, it didn't hurt anymore. Living sacrifices come close to killing you—but don't. You continue to live with the pain.

"Actually, I don't mind making a sacrifice," I reconsidered, "if I'm sure God wants it. But how am I supposed to know if He does? I feel as if I've got a pile of burnt offerings here that stink to high heavens. No sweet aroma from this altar!"

Then I remembered the overly browned toast I served my husband at breakfast. "I can't do anything right," I sighed.

Shocked by my own frankness, I sat there until the sermon ended. Then I sang the final hymn and slipped out of the church as inconspicuously as possible. I needed time to think.

Listen to the Many Voices

* "If you're not willing to sacrifice everything you've got, you're really not following Christ. Those who hold back are not true disciples."

* "Your ministry must come before everything. Where you place it shows how much you love your Lord."

* "If your sacrifice isn't hurting, you're probably not in the perfect will of God. It costs to follow Christ."

* "If your sacrifice is hurting, you're not supposed to show it. Be joyful about giving up things for your Lord."

All voices in unison: "Be willing to sacrifice everything for your ministry: your possessions, your health, your family, and your friendships. These are nice but temporal. Only kingdom work is eternal."

Our response: "I guess I'm a second-rate Christian. It's killing me to sacrifice—to give up personal goals and family time for ministry. It's not that I don't love the Lord. I do and with all my heart. But are all these sacrifices necessary?"

A Lone Voice: "You're listening to others again. Why don't you sort through the voices and pick what comes from Me?"

Accentuating the Positive

I turned the key, opened the door, dragged my suitcases inside, and turned the lock. Home at last! Exhausted, I slumped into a chair at the kitchen table. I felt tears welling up in my eyes.

"Why am I doing this?" I asked myself. "Why am I sharing a gospel that all don't want to hear? Why do I continue to listen as women pour out their problems, knowing their needs are greater than my ability to meet them? Why do I put up with impossible schedules, unreliable airlines, and lonely hotel rooms? Why?

"I've got problems enough without creating more. Spinal arthritis that dogs me with pain. A mother dying of Alzheimer's. A businessman husband whom I dearly love but who travels more than he should. And kids and grandkids I don't get to see grow up because they're scattered all over the country."

By this time my emotions were spilling out. I reached for a box of Kleenex and spotted a note from my husband. Tucked under a cassette, it read, "I love you, Jeep. It was hard to leave knowing I wouldn't be snuggling up to you for awhile. But I'll call tonight. By the way, this tape blessed me. You might want to listen to it in your spare time. Love, Lee."

"Spare time!" I snapped. "What spare time?" Nevertheless, I slipped the tape into the player and began to unpack. The speaker was a man known for his flat-out commitment to the Lord Jesus Christ. He is one of my favorites, and my husband knew that.

"God wants people who are sold out to Him," the tape began. "A person who is not totally committed can be a liability to the kingdom of God. A Christian, by the nature of his name, is one who has decided to follow Christ regardless."

True.

"But there is a cost to discipleship," the preacher continued.

Ah, yes.

"Jesus told His disciples, 'Anyone who loves his father, mother, son, or daughter more than me is not worthy of me.' Then he said, 'If anyone would come after me, he must deny himself and take up his cross daily and follow me.'

"Excuses won't do: 'Permit me first to go and await the death of my father. First let me go back and say good-bye to my family.' Jesus said, 'No one who puts his hand to the plow and looks back is fit for service in the kingdom of God.' Although salvation is free, the price of living the Christian life obediently can be very high indeed."

Tell me about it!

"The value a Christian places on ministry can be an indication of how much he loves the Lord," the tape played on. "Think of those who have given their lives that the gospel might go forth." (Here the preacher mentioned names.) "What role models for those of us who feel weak in our faith!"

Talk on. Convince me.

"There are times when we think we're alone" (the voice was softening now). "But we aren't. We have the Holy Spirit to comfort and sustain us. He is always there—to heal our hurts, fill our emptiness, and cushion the criticism others make."

"I know these things are true," I mused, stopping the tape. "So what's wrong with me? Why am I such a reluctant servant of the Lord I dearly love?"

I turned the tape back on, hoping for balance to the exhortations I had just heard. It came. As best I could, I filtered it through the pressures Christian women are feeling.

Overstatement and Truth

* *The FCW thinks,* "All sacrifices made in the name of the Lord are good ones."

The Lone Voice whispers, "Careful! By thinking this way you can hurt yourself and a lot of other people as well. In fact, without realizing it, you can even hurt the kingdom of God, the very thing you want to help. What the Lord wants from you is not your broken health or your broken relationships but, rather, your broken heart—a heart that has been shattered by pressures and stress and now wants to be made whole, this time beating not with man's demands but with God's desires.

* *The FCW thinks,* "There are times when I know I'm sacrificing my marriage, my kids, my friendships, even my health in order to continue my ministry. But I have to keep going because this is what commitment is all about."

The Lone Voice whispers, "Who said? Without your health, marriage, kids, and friends, you may not have a ministry. The Christian whose house is not in order brings little credence to the gospel.

"But your problem seems to go deeper. You seem to be equating dedication to your ministry with your commitment to God. They are not the same. To confuse them is to fracture you and your relationship with others as well."

* *The FCW thinks*, "I'm not hurting enough on this one. I must be outside God's perfect will."

The Lone Voice whispers, "Where did you get the idea that if it hurts, you're doing what God wants, and if it doesn't, you're not? The Bible says, 'To obey is better than sacrifice' (1 Sam. 15:22). It's a question of just doing what God commands, whether it hurts, brings joy, or does neither.

"For example, Abraham was instructed to sacrifice his only son. What pain! The Israelites were asked to give of their wealth to build Solomon's temple. What joy! Moses was commanded to lay down his staff. Neither joy nor pain, this was just obedience. But obedience—or the willingness to be obedient—was what God required. His will had nothing to do with pain or the extent of it. The same is true today."

* *The FCW thinks*, "I'm hurting, but I can't admit it. Really spiritual people never hurt."

The Lone Voice whispers, "Wrong. God's Son wept at the tomb of Lazarus and sweat drops of blood in the Garden of Gethsemane. If you're hurting, feel free to admit it. Then let God snuggle you into His arms and hold you close—so close you can feel the beat of His love."

A Divine Perspective

One day as I was studying the ministry of Jesus, I came upon the familiar account of His anointing at Bethany. "A woman came with an alabaster jar of very expensive perfume . . . " I read, "and poured [it] on his head" (Mark 14:3).

As I tried to picture this event, several things struck me. First, I noted, the woman chose not the customary olive oil with which to do her anointing, but "pure nard." This was a costly scent, worth about a year's wages. "We have a real sacrifice here!" I surmised.

Then I read that the woman broke the jar; efficiently she then poured out the perfume. She obviously wasn't satisfied with "a little dab'll do ya." She was giving her all, emptying the liquid on Jesus' head. The effect was wonderful: the fragrance of perfume filled the whole house.

"What an expression of love!" I thought. Immediately my mind raced back in time to a situation I hadn't thought about for years. It was spring. Our twins, who were avid coin collectors, were about to celebrate their tenth birthdays; and as far as I knew, Jeff hadn't purchased anything for his twin brother Greg.

Not wanting Greg to be disappointed, I approached Jeff and asked, "Do you want me to do your shopping for you?"

"Don't worry, Mom," he assured me. "It's under control. Trust me."

Well, I wanted to, but I couldn't help being anxious as the big day got closer. Finally, it arrived, complete with balloons, cake, candles, and gifts.

When all the presents on the table had been opened, I watched as Jeff took a very small package from his pocket. He presented it to his brother. Eagerly Greg slid off the ribbon and ripped open the paper. As he lifted the top of the small box, he gasped. So did I.

There in the cotton was Jeff's most valuable coin. "Wow!" Greg exclaimed, expressing the sentiment of all of us. "Wow!"

Later I got Jeff alone. "What you did today was special," I said. "But I am curious. Out of all the coins in your collection, why did you give Greg your best?"

"Because he is my brother," Jeff replied. Tears welled up in my eyes as I thought of Mary of Bethany.

Back in the here and now, I continued my meditation. Mary was criticized for her actions, I noticed. And the criticism didn't come from those outside religious circles; it came from within. It hurts when it comes from within, I empathized, especially when the rationalization sounds so pious.

"Why this waste of perfume?" the observers asked. "It could have been sold . . . and the money given to the poor" (v. 5). I flipped to the parallel passage in John 12 and noted that Judas was the one who posed the question (see v. 4).

On the surface the question sounded logical, even advisable, and certainly "religious." Mary could have easily listened. But she was listening to another voice and chose to heed it instead.

She had saved this perfume for the day of Jesus' burial, John tells us, but came to a decision to use it while Jesus was still alive. It was to be a living sacrifice, much more valuable than a dead one.

"She has done a beautiful thing to me," Jesus said (Mark 14:6).

Amazing! A few minutes earlier Mary was being rebuked. Now she was being acclaimed. Disapproval and approval for the same action. But if Jesus approves, I mused, does it matter if others disapprove?

The next thing that struck me was the far-reaching effect of Mary's sacrifice. "Wherever the gospel is preached throughout the world," Jesus went on to say, "what she has done will be told" (v. 9).

"Wow!" I exclaimed, borrowing the expression from my son Greg. "This woman had no idea of the impact she was making and the extent to which its ramifications would go. Do any of us?"

As I pondered these things in my heart, I was strangely warmed. But I was quickly brought back to reality by the cold facts of the next verse: "Then Judas Iscariot went to the chief priests to betray Jesus to them" (v. 10).

It was hard to believe. Here was a man who had had fellowship with the Master for three soul-stirring years. Now he was willing to give it all up for a mere thirty pieces of silver!

Two sacrifices: one good, one bad. One pleased the Lord and displeased the religious leaders; the other pleased the leaders and wounded the Lord.

No doubt Judas thought his sacrifice was a good one. After all, it was what the religious community wanted. He probably figured he would be held in esteem because of it. But when he wasn't— when he realized the chief priests weren't concerned about him personally, that all they wanted was his sacrifice—he was devastated.

Then he saw the awful consequences: Jesus was being sentenced to death! That was it. He couldn't live with himself any longer. So he "went away and hanged himself" (Matt. 27:5).

Emotionally, I was there. I pictured the Middle East sun as it rose in the morning sky. I watched as its rays struck the body, suspended from a branch by a rope. All day long the corpse hung there, rotting in the humid air. The odor must have been unbearable! Far different from the fragrance of a life poured out in love, this was the stench of death.

For awhile I just sat in my chair, speechless. I had never connected these two events before. And I had never seen Judas's betrayal as a "sacrifice." But there it was. As I contemplated it, I remembered my own pile of "burnt offerings," and I knew I had to make some changes.

What Can We Do to Change Things?

Judge each criticism in the light of God's will. If we're being criticized wrongly (for doing that which is right), it's wise to reach for blinders and earmuffs and continue to "run the race," focusing on the Coach—and only on the Coach—and proceed to the finish line. If, however, we're being criticized rightly (for doing that which is wrong), it's wise to stop running altogether, sit down, check the Rule Book, and start over, this time doing things according to the Author's instructions.

Ask the Lord for discernment concerning sacrifice. "I want to give all You require, Father. But please let me know what it is. I don't want to give up things for the wrong purpose."

Before we go any further, let's pause to heed a warning. Any time believers pray for spiritual discernment, they strike a nerve in the kingdom of darkness. It's time for the deceiver to move in and try to block the light.

Not about to announce his arrival with a fanfare of trumpets, the enemy usually appears without even a name tag. He doesn't extend his right hand and say, "Good morning! I'm Satan. Pleased to meet you." Instead, he knocks on the back door, masquerading as a trusted friend. "Want a deeper spiritual walk?" he asks. "Let's chat."

Remember his temptation to Eve in the Garden of Eden? Enticing her to taste the forbidden fruit, he crooned, "God knows that when you eat of it, your eyes will be opened, and you will be like God, knowing good and evil" (Gen. 3:4). Here was a promise of spiritual discernment. Eve wanted that. So she gave in. And she received spiritual blindness instead.

"You want to be a godly Christian role model?" I can hear the enemy ask. "Then make some really good sacrifices. And make sure everybody knows about them. The more you give up, the more spiritual you are, you know."

His voice is one among many. Unfortunately, his voice can come through the many. So we specifically watch for false messages, tune them out, and tune into the only voice that counts.

Have no preconceptions about the worth of a sacrifice. Giving up something dear in order to do the Lord's work does not automatically place us within the will of God. By the same token, if we feel we haven't really sacrificed to do the Lord's work, that does not automatically indicate balance. It is wise to assess each opportunity individually, subjecting it to the scrutiny of God's Word and the wisdom of godly advisors.

Take a personal inventory of sacrifices made. Get a pencil and paper, and let's make a list of what we gave up within the last year in order to do "church work" (time alone, time with family, etc.). Now, let's go down the list, item by item, asking,

1. Was this sacrifice worth it?
2. Did I make this sacrifice because
   a. God required it?
   b. I assumed God required it?
   c. others led me to believe God required it?
   d. I just wanted to?
3. Did this sacrifice make me feel
   a. godly?
   b. proud?
   c. accepted?
   d. empty?
4. Was the godliness false? the pride harmful? the acceptance worth it? the emptiness productive?

When hurting, unload—but in the right places. As Jesus was agonizing on the cross, bearing the burden of our sins, He looked to heaven. "Father," He cried, "into Your hands I commit my spirit" (Luke 23:46). Then He was ushered into the presence of God. There He was graciously received, His sacrifice accepted, His burden relieved—all in a way that could not be duplicated.

God will do the same for us. When we go to Him with our burdens, He receives us, He accepts us, He comforts us in a way nobody else can. This is not to say He cannot minister to us by means other than a direct encounter. He can and He does. But why bother to go elsewhere when we can go directly to the Source of comfort Himself?

Sometimes, however, we feel the need to dump on somebody besides the Lord: somebody with "skin on 'em." It's a human longing. Whether the person we choose is a pastor, a counselor, or a friend, we want someone we can trust, someone who is spiritually mature, and someone who will listen without judging. We have every right to expect our confidante, once chosen, to consult the Word of God, pray both for us and with us, and "with meekness and fear" advise us what to do—all of this while holding our trust in confidence. It is an awesome request. But it can be a wise one. Other people can see things we cannot see and help us in ways we cannot help ourselves. They can be valuable sources of comfort— physical and emotional as well as spiritual.

Families can help, too. Try throwing out the question, "Hey, kids, what do you think about Mom's being gone so much?" Then brace yourself for the answer. Chances are, they'll "tell it like it is," even if nobody else has the courage. God's truth often comes "out of the mouths of babes." From experience we know it can come from the mouths of husbands, too! Not only can these family members help us see ourselves as others see us, but their advice is cheap—so don't tell them some people charge for doing what they, family members, have just done.

Confirmation from God's Word

1. Read Judges 11:29–40 aboutJephthah's vow.
2. Ponder:
   - What vow does Jephthah make to the Lord (vv. 30–31)?
   - Why does he make it?
   - In what ways is this a "rash" vow?
   - Why does Jephthah feel compelled to keep his vow (see Eccl. 5:4–7)?
   - How many people suffer because of Jephthah's sacrifice?
   - Who do you think suffers the most?
   - Do you think God was pleased with Jephthah's sacrifice? Why or why not?

3. What steps can the FCW take to keep from making a sacrifice that is not only outside the will of God but harmful to her family and unnecessarily painful to herself?

What care I who gets the credit?
  Only let the work be done.
Christ Himself will handle credits
With the setting of the sun.
—Ralph S. Cushmen, from "Credits"

7

I Can't Measure Up!

When they measure themselves by themselves
and compare themselves with themselves, they are not wise.
2 Corinthians 10:12

Brenda decided to sit down and watch a few minutes of TV while she folded the laundry. Finding the set already tuned to a Christian channel, she figured she'd leave it there. The program in progress was a talk show, with an anchorwoman interviewing a best-selling author.

"That's an attractive hairstyle," Brenda remarked, studying the anchor carefully. "I wonder how it would look on me."

The camera shifted to the guest, whose conversation with the anchor was beginning to intensify. Brenda noticed how well the author was expressing herself. "Why can't I be articulate?" she wondered. "I bumble all over the place."

Soon another guest was introduced—a Bible teacher of some renown. She looked lovely in her navy outfit, dark stockings, and matching heels. Brenda remembered her own navy suit which shrank with its last cleaning (at least that's what she liked to think). "When I get my next paycheck," she decided, "I'll shop for a new one—a size larger."

The next TV guest was an evangelist. He was good-looking, neat, and self-confident. Soon all four were discussing methods of reaching people for Christ.

"You have to awaken a need," the evangelist contributed, "if you want to have a response. People won't reach out for bread until they recognize they're hungry."

"True," Brenda agreed, thinking of the testimony she'd be giving at her women's meeting. "I really want God to use me to save souls."

"You've got to be aggressive," the author insisted. "Create openings. Hand out tracts. Small pamphlets that have a salvation prayer at the end can be used in groups as well as with individuals."

"I'm not comfortable reading a tract," she thought. "Too canned. Yet if it brings results, I might be tempted to try it."

"When I am invited to speak at evangelistic functions," the Bible teacher remarked, "I ask every guest to fill out a comment card. Those who want to know how to have a personal relationship with God are asked to mark an 'X' on the card."

"That's a good idea," Brenda concurred as she increased the volume with her remote control. "With comment cards people can indicate an interest in spiritual things without feeling embarrassed."

"What's wrong with a public call—asking inquirers to come down front?" the evangelist inserted. "It singles out the serious from the not-so-serious."

"Well, I'm certainly not going to do that," Brenda exclaimed to herself. "It's too exposed—for both the inquirer and the speaker. What if nobody walked forward? And what if somebody did? What would I do next?"

As the TV discussion continued, Brenda found herself becoming more and more engrossed. She was sorry to see the clock ticking away, signaling the final minutes of the program.

"We all want to be used by God," the anchor summarized. "Our question is which one gets the best results? Is it appearance? Approach? Presentation? Techniques? Or a combination? We have been privileged to listen to some very successful people—all recognized in their fields. Now, the challenge is to implement these suggestions in our own lives, for all of us want to be Christians who make an impact on our world."

"I certainly do," Brenda admitted. "But at what cost? How much am I willing to try?" She weighed her options.

Then she stopped short. "If I were to achieve success as most

Christians view it, would I necessarily be successful in the eyes of God?" She knew she had to weigh that question seriously.

But there were other questions as well. Is God as impressed with numbers as His people are? What does God think when Carrie covets Connie's hairdo or Brian borrows a technique that works for Bob? Brenda was troubled, deeply troubled, as she struggled with the messages she was receiving.

Listen to the Many Voices

* "Numbers are an indication of a successful ministry. The more heads you can count, the better you're doing."

* "Compare your outreach to more successful ones. If it doesn't measure up, make changes. Success is the name of the game."

* "If you receive no recognition, you're not being effective. When your ministry is having an impact, it'll be known."

All voices in unison: "Gauge the success of your ministry by concrete evidence. If you can't see results, there probably aren't any."

Our response: "I can't measure up. My spiritual trophy case is empty. The success of others seems out of my reach. And most of the people I try to help don't even bother to thank me. Call me a failure, because that's what I am."

A Lone Voice: "You feel that way because you're being influenced by voices other than Mine. Listen to Me—and only to Me—and you will be set free from the destructive effects of comparison."

Accentuating the Positive

As a member of the Christian Education Committee, I was attending an evaluation meeting for Sunday School teachers. After opening the session in prayer and thanking us for our participation in a successful program, the superintendent asked, "How has the year gone for each of you?"

What followed were the usual complaints about student rowdiness and apathy. Then the superintendent requested comments that were positive—comments that would encourage us.

Margot spoke first. A columnist for our church newsletter, she had the reputation of being a model teacher. Every hair in place, flawless makeup, turned-up collar, and hose that matched her shoes—all gave the impression that here was someone who attended to detail. "Our class has grown by 32 percent," she reported. "But more important, we've witnessed spiritual growth." An envious groan swept through the room.

Cheryl rose next. Known for her tender heart and compassionate outreach, she reported having recruited several students from dysfunctional families. "In Ashley's case we prayed that her parents wouldn't get a divorce," she said. "So far so good. In fact, last Sunday Ashley ran up and gave me a hug. 'I love you, Teach,' she said. It was a perfect ending to a great year." We clapped our praises to God.

Charlie was the next contributor. In real estate sales, he was used to bringing opportunities to closure. "Three of my students came to Christ this year," he announced. Then he asked, "How many converts did the rest of you have?"

Several teachers shifted uneasily in their seats. Then Doris spoke up. Usually quiet and not at all assertive, she surprised us by stating, "I can't speak for anybody else, but I don't give invitations. This is not to say I don't present the gospel. I do. But I feel the saving of souls is God's job, not mine. He's the only One who knows the true results anyway."

An "Amen" reverberated from one corner of the room and was quickly echoed. At this point the superintendent scrambled to end the evening on a harmonious note. He was successful.

But the discussion wasn't over for me. In fact, it had just begun. I knew that fractured Christian women everywhere are being negatively pressured by remarks like Charlie's, so I made an appointment to speak with a pastor who was known for his straight-forward, biblical answers. Here is part of our dialogue, that afternoon:

Peg: Pastor, does it ever bother you that Christians are being pressured to produce visible results of their ministries? To grow in numbers? To count heads? To take tallies of those who receive Christ? Do you think God is impressed with our numbers?

Pastor: No, but God does not disregard numbers altogether. After all, He gave us a book of the Bible with that title. He ordered the Israelites to take a census—to count heads, so to speak. So to take attendance or to make a list of converts is not an act of disobedience. In fact, tallies can serve useful purposes.

Peg: But they force Christians to do things they normally wouldn't do, just to get results. I have trouble with this because visible evidence is not necessarily an indication of how active God has been.

Pastor: Of course it isn't. But it can be one measure of effectiveness. When a person raises a hand during an invitation to receive Christ, gives a compliment about a lesson, or expresses thanks for help, it should be taken in good faith that God has done a work, at least until proven otherwise.

Peg: But doesn't the pressure to produce results foster competition between members of the same team, so to speak?

Pastor: It can, but let's not forget a lot can be gained by observing others in ministry, good as well as bad.

(We both laughed.)

Peg: One more comment, Pastor. Some of the most effective Christians I know receive little recognition for their work.

Pastor: True. That's why it's best to commit our ministries to a sovereign God. He knows what has been accomplished because He is the One who has done it.

Peg: I needed that. Thanks, Pastor. You've pointed out what is correct about the pressure to produce results. But from your wisdom I've also gained insight into what is not correct. Now I've got to race home and get it all on paper.

Overstatement and Truth

* *The FCW thinks,* "I don't have any converts to boast of. Therefore I'm unsuccessful in my ministry."

The Lone Voice whispers, "No ministry rendered in the name of the Lord is unsuccessful. It may appear that way, but only to those who focus on results. If you focus on the task at hand and do it for God—and Him alone—you'll be successful every time."

* *The FCW thinks,* "I will copy the ministry techniques of people who are successful. Then maybe I'll get results."

The Lone Voice whispers, "Forget results. Be yourself. Your talents, personality, past experiences, and present opportunities all come together under one banner: unique. Use them creatively. Be free."

* *The FCW thinks,* "I'm not being recognized for what I'm

doing for God. Therefore, I'm ineffective."

The Lone Voice whispers, "Who said recognition is an indication of effectiveness? This thinking produces self-promoters, performers, even manipulators. Just be faithful to what God has called you to do and in His eyes—which are the only eyes that count—you will be a success."

A Divine Perspective

I had been asked to conduct a workshop on sharing our faith, and I was nervous. "I'm not qualified," I argued. "Ask somebody else—somebody who's an expert in this field—somebody who's aggressive, articulate, and ready with answers. There will be lots of questions, you know, and I won't measure up to people's expectations."

"Don't give excuses; just do it," the Lord seemed to say as He led me to 1 Corinthians, chapter 3. "I'll tell you what to say."

Wanting to be obedient, I prayed, "Lord, make me willing to be willing." Then I started to read. As I did, I found I was bringing to Scripture a smattering of background information. The Corinthian church was rent with problems. One was the tendency of members to become enamored with their leaders. "We follow Paul," one group was saying. Another, "We follow Apollos." A third, waxing spiritual, was boasting, "We follow Christ!"

"Well, I follow Christ too," I said to myself, "but deliver me from becoming so self-righteous about it." Then I remembered the times I had coveted the gifts of others so I could share in their acclaim. "Hey, I'm no better than these Corinthians," I realized.

I read on. "What, after all, is Apollos? And what is Paul? Only servants through whom you come to believe" (v. 5). "Servants," I repeated as the implications sank in. "We're servants! Servants are people in no position to covet or boast. They're just expected to do what their Master commands for His acclaim, not theirs."

I continued my reading. "The Lord has assigned to each his task." Since our son Jeff had just treated us to a tour of the automobile assembly plant where he was employed, these words brought back vivid images of what I witnessed there. First of all, I was impressed with the orderliness of the process. There was clearly someone in charge, for each worker had a job to do and each was busy doing it—at least while we were looking. Nobody was running from one task to another. Everybody was fairly stationary, concentrating on doing only one thing, as the FCW in me took notice.

Some workers were welding frames, others were installing wiring, while still others were adjusting glass. Throughout the whole plant tasks were being accomplished. I noticed some tasks were more glamorous than others. A few of the workers with these glamorous jobs had developed quite a flair for performing them. Those were the ones I stopped to watch. But as a potential owner of one of these vehicles, I found myself appreciating the contribution of each and every worker. Nobody was superfluous in this operation! And if anyone was coveting another's position or flair, it wasn't obvious to me.

I did notice, however, that if one worker got distracted and subsequently fouled up, the whole line shut down. Fortunately, this didn't happen very often, Jeff informed us. Usually, the car-in-the-making got put together. And someone at the end of the line slid into the driver's seat and started the ignition. The first time I watched this happen, I thought I was witnessing a miracle (the workers may have thought so too, but nobody said anything).

"One plants the seed," the apostle Paul said. "Another waters. But God makes it grow."

"Yes, He does!" I confirmed. He's the One running the assembly line."

Then I read, "So neither he who plants nor he who waters is anything, but only God, who makes things grow" (v. 7).

"Thank You, Lord," I exclaimed. "Getting an end result is not my job. It's Yours! I can't make things happen the way I want to anyway. So thanks for saying I don't have to. But I can be faithful. I can contribute my part. And I can do so without coveting and without feeling the need to receive recognition. I wouldn't even be on the assembly line if You hadn't chosen me. So I want all the acclaim to go to the intelligence behind this operation. You deserve it.

"I must say, though, I can't wait to witness a miracle. I can't wait to see a car I had a part in building suddenly spring to life. I can't wait to watch it move out into the world, drawing on the power within. What a tribute to everybody in the plant! And what a tribute to You, our Supervisor!"

I continued my reading. "The man who plants and the man

who waters have one purpose" (to reap a harvest, I deduced; "to produce an automobile that runs and runs well," I translated). But it was the end of the verse that gripped me: "and each will be rewarded according to his own labor" (v. 8).

"According to his own labor," I mused, "not according to the end result! The car doesn't even have to be finished! The workers still get 'paid.' Results are God's business, since He's running the line. But faithfulness is our business, since we're in His employ."

At this point I felt like screaming, "Hallelujah!" But it's not in my upbringing to do so, so I kept quiet, at least for the moment.

Then the impact of the passage hit me: I am free—free to be me! I no longer have to measure up—not to anybody's standard but God's. He's my Boss, my only Boss. But His standard is one of excellence. So I'd better read the Instruction Manual again and ask the Supervisor to explain it. I don't want to foul up and stop that line.

As people-in-process pass my way, I want to be sensitive to their each and every need. Should I contribute this part or that? Do they need more than one piece of information, or did the last worker dump on too much? When I'm satisfied I've done what is required, I will cheerfully release the unfinished souls to the workers stationed farther down the line. My particular job is done.

Excitement was welling up within me. I could feel it. "I can't wait to share these findings at my workshop!" I thought. "But the workshop is weeks away. I could explode by then!" So to let off steam, I shut the back door, and right there in my kitchen, in the heartiest voice I could muster, I shouted, "Hallelujah!"

Then I sat down at the table to put it all on paper.

What Can We Do to Change Things?

Refuse to be caught in the comparison trap. Each one of us is special, a combination of 60 trillion cells that have come together in a way they will never come together again. There's only one you. There's only one me. Aren't you glad?

Although most of us come equipped with eyes, ears, mouth, hands, feet, and a variety of inner parts, that's where the similarity stops. Different in body chemistry, carriage, personality, experience, and opportunity, we present ourselves uniquely. Our voices become signatures, complete with inflections, vocal twirls, and measured emphases. Those who know us can recognize who we are without even seeing us. On the phone it takes only one word and I hear, "Hi, Peg."

Mannerisms give us away, too. Who else peers out from under her eyelashes and melts the hardest heart? Who else strikes a model's pose whenever a camera appears? Who else giggles infectiously at nothing in particular? In each case, just one precious daughter-in-law—and I'll never tell which one.

This concept of personal uniqueness was brought home to me while on a speaking tour in California. Beginning in Santa Barbara, I was to work my way down to San Diego. Each group I was to address would present a fashion show. Models would strut down carpeted ramps, displaying gorgeous clothes, some one-of-a-kind, contributed by movie stars. I loved every outfit I saw. When I discovered the prices, I loved them even more.

The minute the first show was over, I raced to the back room and made my selections quickly. By the time I got to my second engagement, my suitcase was already bulging. No room for even a hankie. So I couldn't allow myself the luxury of even a look at what was being offered. Temptation came, however, in the person of Rose. She was running the show.

"I've got a black velvet suit back there," she signaled, "that I think would look stunning on you."

"Don't tempt me, Rose," I cautioned. "I can't fit another thing into my bag."

"Well, just come look at it," she persuaded.

So I did. I noticed the outfit consisted of three pieces: a jacket, a skirt, and pants. I ran my hand over the velvet; it was deep, dark, and lush. Down the side of the jacket I discovered a label. My heart began to race. This was a "designer original." Hesitantly, I turned over the price tag: $30.

"Why don't you just try it on?" Rose suggested.

"Why not?" I rationalized. "I don't have to buy it."

The pants didn't fit. "That does it," I said convincingly. "I'm not supposed to have this suit. See?"

"No problem," Rose assured me. "I'll sell the pants separately. Then you can have the suit for twenty dollars."

Now, what would you do if you were offered a designer original for only twenty dollars but couldn't get it into your suitcase? Let me tell you what I did: I contributed what I had been wearing to the shop sponsoring the fashion show. Then I walked on stage in my new black suit, which, by the way, Rose had given me for ten dollars since I had made a contribution to the cause.

I wore that suit with pride. It was unlike any other black suit in the whole world (barring cheaper imitations, of course). I knew that, and I wanted everyone else to know it too. So occasionally, I would take off my jacket and position it so the label showed. Why not? That way the designer would get the credit he deserved. After all, it was he who fashioned this garment and assigned its original worth.

Uniqueness, self-esteem, self-worth, self-confidence—all are the gifts of a great Creator, One who shuns poorly constructed imitations and goes for the genuine every time. Let's do the same.

Carry out each ministry with a specific purpose in mind. What do we want to see happen: the conversion of a soul? The restoration of a relationship? The healing of a hurt? While only God can accomplish any of these things, we realize He may want to accomplish them through us. So we focus, not trying to do His work for Him, yet not letting Him move without us either. We're co-workers with our Maker, confident in His strength, relying on His power. Results then come. But they come in God's time and in God's perfect way. They can't be hurried or manipulated. "Impress this truth on our souls, dear Lord," I prayed.

Whether teaching, speaking, counseling, or just plain "helping," use the Word of God. "Don't let me preach at them, Lord, but cloak my words in wisdom, love, and tact," I prayed. Of all the means, methods, and techniques available to contemporary Christians, Scripture is the only thing that carries a guarantee: it will not "return empty." It will "accomplish what God desires and achieve the purpose for which [He] sent it" (Isa. 55:11). Because of this built-in power, we can expect built-in success every time, whether we see outward signs or not.

When conducting a ministry, expect nothing in return. Be grateful for anything that comes. It's the only way to avoid disappointment. Some Christians get paid for what they do; others are expected to serve free of charge. Some get plaques engraved with their names (or even portraits in oil) hung in the church foyer; most are not so recognized. Some receive applause, words of appreciation, or notes of encouragement; others receive nothing. When Jesus healed ten lepers, only one returned to thank Him. Sad to say, that's about par for the Christian world.

Sometimes, however, accolades do come, even to the most undeserving of us. Oh, to receive them with grace and to resist the temptation to think, "I've done something significant." God is the One who has done something significant, and He guards His honor jealously. The challenge to us is to hold our recognition loosely and to save every compliment for when we get alone with our Lord. Then we can present the acclaim to Him, the same way we would a bouquet of beautiful flowers—one that was addressed to Him anyway.

When we do this, the focus of our ministry shifts—to where it belonged in the first place. Jesus is now up front. We are standing behind the cross, and we discover it's not a bad place to be. There's no pressure to look perfect or to perform flawlessly. Everybody's looking at Jesus. He's the object of attention.

When someone sneaks behind the cross and says, "Thanks" (to us, not to Him), we find ourselves blushing with embarrassment. Or when somebody gives us credit for "our" ministries, we find ourselves pointing upward. The focus is now on Jesus Christ. We're not even tempted anymore. We have become spectators to a divine drama. And the remarkable thing is that we love it!

Confirmation from God's Word

1. Read Luke 17:5–10 regarding the "unprofitable" servant.
2. Ponder verses 7–10:
    • For whom was the servant working? Himself or another?
    • Was he applauded for his service?
    • How do you think he felt when, instead of being recognized for a day's work ("Come along now and sit down to eat"), he was asked to perform yet another task?
    • In what sense is he "unworthy" of praise?
    • In what sense did he only do his "duty"?
3. Note: The flip side of "faith" (v. 5) is "faithfulness." Keeping this in mind, how much "faith" does one need to accomplish things for God (see v. 6)? How much "faithfulness"? On whose faithfulness does the accomplishment of a task rely? The Master's? The servant's? Both?
4. What message is there in this passage for the FCW?

*hy is it that Christianity,
which promises
to forgive and heal guilt,
sometimes seems to bring on more?*
—*Tim Stafford*[7]

8

This Guilt Is Killing Me!

*Rejoice in the Lord and be glad, you righteous;
sing, all you who are upright in heart.*
Psalm 32:11

I took my window seat over the plane's wing. It was going to be a rough forty hours on this "milk run" to Australia. I could feel the tension building.

My sponsoring group had scheduled me tightly. With fifty lectures to give in only six weeks, I would have little time for personal matters. This worried me. Plus, adjusting to a significant time change and a different culture would be a challenge. I was apprehensive.

I was also feeling guilty. Mother's health was deteriorating, and I was about to embark on a trip that would take me halfway around the world. I would be unable to get to her quickly should there be an emergency.

Mental videos of the last few days started replaying in my head. My sisters Polly and Diane and I (with the help of husbands) had moved Mother from the "assisted living area" to the Alzheimer's wing of a life care facility in Massachusetts. The move involved dividing up furniture and clothes she couldn't take with her.

"You take this," Polly had said as she sorted through Mother's costume jewelry. "No, you take it," Diane replied as she turned her attention to scarves. I looked up from my drawer of belts. Tears were streaming down my sisters' cheeks. Here we were, dividing up our "inheritance," and Mother hadn't even died yet. But then I remembered Jesus hadn't either when the soldiers cast lots for His robe. Ugh!

When we finished with the clothes, we met with the doctor to request that when the time came, "no extraordinary means" be used to extend Mother's life. Then it was time to say good-bye and begin the six-hour drive home.

As Diane and I walked upstairs, I tried to focus on the good things the weekend had to offer. We had reminisced about Mother's days on the farm, and her eyes had come alive as she remembered. We had taken her to a favorite restaurant and then for a beautiful drive in the country. We had even wheeled her through the mall so she could enjoy the decorations. She had sung "Jingle Bells" to the background music. Our hearts were warmed—at least for a while.

Then Mother looked up at the one guiding her wheelchair and asked, "Who are you?"

"I'm Peggy, your oldest daughter," I replied. I could see the vacant eyes trying to focus and the brain cells attempting to pull it all together.

"You are not!" she concluded emphatically. "You don't even look like her. And you don't sound like her either. Peggy is much younger than you." I could hear my sisters muffling giggles. In situations like this you either laugh or cry. We had opted to laugh.

"Maybe saying good-bye this time won't be so bad after all," I thought. "Mother is pretty far gone." How wrong I was. When Diane and I entered her room, she looked up. Then this woman, who hadn't recognized any of us for months, addressed my sister by her nickname. "Dido," she pleaded, "please take me home."

The words cut through us like a knife. Gently, we both bent down to kiss her, then arranged her hospital garment over her frail frame. "We love you," we said. And with a pat we turned to go. Once we did, we never looked back. We couldn't. The decision to leave her had been made. That all happened yesterday.

Today was a new day, and I was on my way to a brand new challenge. But I couldn't shake loose my guilt. In fact, it intensified as I mentally enumerated decisions my friends had made on behalf of their ailing parents. Judy had cared for her mother at home, almost until her death. Betty had checked her father into a facility nearby so she could visit him often. When Vivian's mother became ill, Vivian gave up her job. And Nancy told me she had asked the doctors to employ whatever means necessary to extend her stepmother's life. As I weighed these decisions, I became increasingly disturbed. My sisters were being haunted too, I would discover later.

"But why are we blaming ourselves for the predicament Mother is in?" I questioned. In fact, we had little to do with it. She checked herself into the Massachusetts facility years before she knew she was ill so she would "never become a burden" to her kids. When our family, who at the time was living close to her, got transferred out of state, Mother elected to stay where she was. When we girls discussed the demands of our professions in the light of her deteriorating health, she urged us to continue pursuing our careers. And when the discussion turned to extraordinary life support, she expressed her desire to die with dignity. These decisions were Mother's. So why were we feeling guilty?

As I struggled to come up with an answer, I thought back over other occasions when I had been overwhelmed with misplaced guilt: the numerous times I had thrown away financial requests from legitimate Christian organizations because there was no way we could meet the needs of the whole world! The time we were forced to drop the support of a missionary in order to handle a more urgent need at home. The time I said no to serving on a church committee because I was too strung out doing other things. The time we had to return a foreign missionary's daughter to her parents when the live-in arrangement didn't work out. And the time I skipped Bible study because I had to clean the house for a weekend guest. I even felt guilty when I let the cat out and it was run over by the mail truck.

In some of these cases, I may have made the wrong decision and, therefore, should have felt guilty. But in every case I did what I felt was right at the time; and given the same set of circumstances, I would probably do the same thing again. Yet guilt remained. Why?

Can it be that sometimes we are made to feel guilty when in fact we are not? Do voices of condemnation come from people who haven't walked in our shoes yet feel they should judge us as if they had? Does the most painful criticism come from people we admire and, therefore, we give it more credence? Is the "accuser of the brothers" (the one with the plan to lead the whole world astray) working overtime (see Rev. 12:9–10)?

If we are aware of these traps, shouldn't we be able to avoid misplaced guilt? Especially when it's associated with a legitimate refusal to take on an obligation? Yet for some reason, we become entangled by what we are hearing.

Listen to the Many Voices

* "Go through every door God opens. If He didn't want you to go through them, He wouldn't be opening them."

* "If you say no to a Christian opportunity, feel guilty, really guilty. After all, you are saying no to an opportunity to serve your Lord."

* "God expects you to use your abilities, talents, and gifts for His glory. Failure to do so will cause your skills to atrophy. Then you will be 'shelved.'"

All voices in unison: "Do more for God. If you're holding back, you're 'luke-warm,' and God will 'spit you out of His mouth'" (see Rev. 3:16).

Our response: "It scares me when people talk like that. I know I fall short of God's standards. But I also know that if I confess my sins, God is 'faithful and just' to forgive my sins and purify me from all unrighteousness. So why am I still feeling guilty?"

A Lone Voice: "You are letting the voices of others control you—not only how you act but how you feel. Why don't you listen to My voice and let me be the controlling influence in your life?"

Accentuating the Positive

As I packed up our books from the marriage seminar, I heard a male voice ask my husband for counseling.

"We are Bible teachers, not licensed counselors," Lee

informed the man and woman, "but we'd be happy to share informally. Here, pull up two chairs and make yourselves comfortable. Now, what seems to be the problem?"

"Priorities," Dan blurted. "I became a Christian about three years ago, and I love serving the Lord. But I find myself at the church almost every night. There's no time for recreation, TV, or even my wife." With this my ears perked up and I joined the group.

"Yes," Sandi asserted, "and it's affecting our marriage. We both work, you see. And I'm as heavily involved in the church as Dan is. We want to start a family but, honestly, there isn't time. . . . "

"Talk about guilt-city!" Dan sighed.

"Sandi, are you as new to Christianity as your husband?" I inquired.

"No," she answered. "I grew up in the church. I know the pressures it can put on family life."

"Then you also know that when one has been entrusted with many talents, much is required—within reason, of course," Lee interjected.

"We both know that," Dan interrupted. "The willing and able have to pick up the slack. And Sandi and I are willing and able. But when is enough enough?"

"Let me ask you a question," Lee suggested, "and this is not to put more pressure on you—you've got enough of that already—but do you get blessed when you are serving the Lord?"

"Of course," Dan exclaimed. "So much so that even thinking of saying no brings guilt!"

"Okay, let's look at the positive," Lee ventured, shifting in his seat. "As Christians, we are not without an Advisor. We can say to God, 'Is there a reason why You have opened another door at this time in my life? Do You really want me to go through it?'

"If the answer is affirmative and we refuse, then there's reason to feel guilty. We have disobeyed."

"We know that," Sandi articulated. "That's why we say yes so often. We don't want to be like Moses, who was denied access to the promised land."

"Or like Jonah, who got swallowed by a fish," Dan laughed. "Sandi would die of claustrophobia."

"Even the apostle Paul expressed a fear of being disqualified from the race he was running to win," Lee reminded us.

"That's what adds to our guilt," Dan concluded.

"But what if we ask God what we should do and He says 'Cut back on your Christian service'? We have to obey then, too—and without guilt. When we look at all of Scripture as a unified message, we get a balanced view of what God expects. And it's very freeing."

As Lee went through the Scriptures with Dan and Sandi, I listened with the FCW in mind. I found myself becoming increasingly sensitive to the messages we Christian women are hearing.

Overstatement and Truth

* *The FCW thinks*, "I'm expected to go through every door God opens. Open doors are divine mandates."

The Lone Voice whispers, "Who said? Doesn't God have the right to offer you a choice? While there are times when His directives are specific ('Abraham, leave Haran'; 'Jonah, go to Nineveh'), there are other times when He says, 'Go through any door you want.' But rarely does He say, 'Go through every door that's open.' That would cause fracturing."

* *The FCW thinks*, "The guilt I'm feeling for saying no must be coming from God."

The Lone Voice whispers, "Not from God. He sent His Son to enable you to render your services joyfully. Your bondage is coming from yourself or from others, but not from God."

* *The FCW thinks*, "When I'm feeling guilty, I am."

The Lone Voice whispers, "Not necessarily so. It's not that Christians don't sin and shouldn't feel guilty. It's just that there may be no link between the guilt they are feeling and a particular transgression. Search your heart and make a distinction between actual sin and imposed pressure. Then thank the Lord for setting you free."

* *The FCW thinks*, "So I learn to give a sanctified no. But I still have a problem. Just because I know I can say no doesn't mean everybody else knows I can say no. How can I make them appreciate my situation?"

The Lone Voice whispers, "You can't. But you are not responsible for them anyway. You're responsible for you. Just do what is right and leave the consequences to God."

A Divine Perspective

In an effort to get a biblical view of guilt and how it affects us, I turned to the story of King David's encounter with Nathan the prophet (2 Sam. 12). With my vivid imagination, I had no trouble picturing the scene:

"Your majesty," the prophet was stammering, "consider two men: one wealthy, the other poor. The wealthy gentleman owns flocks of sheep and herds of cattle, while the poor man has only one pet lamb, which he loves like a member of his family. It plays with his children, eats from his table, drinks from his cup, and sleeps in his bed.

"One day the rich man invites a guest to dinner. For some reason, instead of slaughtering an animal from his own supply— one that would scarcely be missed—he steals the solitary lamb from the poor man and serves it."

"He deserves to die!" King David declared. "But before he does, he should pay for that lamb four times over."

"You are the man," Nathan stated, pointing his finger in accusation.

"Wow!" I thought. "God must love the king a lot to care enough to confront him with a guilt he's trying to suppress. But what a confrontation! I'm glad I'm not King David."

I knew what the king's sin was. He had committed adultery with Bathsheba; then, in an effort to cover up his sin, he had her husband killed in battle. David was guilty, unquestionably so, of breaking at least two of God's commandments. But it took Nathan's confrontation to bring him to confession.

"Why do we harbor guilt until it almost kills us?" I wondered. "And why do we wait for a confrontation before we decide to do something about it?"

Up to this point I found myself commiserating with King David but not necessarily identifying. After all, I had been faithful to my marriage vows; he hadn't. And I had never taken another's life; he had. I was forced to admit, however, I do entertain my own set of secret sins and from time to time have to seek divine forgiveness.

"I have sinned against the Lord," David confessed. Later he

would chronicle his emotions in a psalm: "There was a time when I wouldn't admit what a sinner I was. But my dishonesty made me miserable . . . I finally admitted all my sins . . . and You [God] forgave me! All my guilt is gone" (Ps. 32:3–5, TLB).

Yes, King David's guilt was gone, not just the fact but the feelings associated with it. There was one hitch though: the consequences of the king's sins remained. That meant the feelings could resurface.

They did with the death of his third son. Overcome with grief, the king cried, "O my son Absalom! My son, my son Absalom! If only I had died instead of you" (2 Sam. 18:33).

As I pondered the king's pain, my mind raced back to his judgment on the rich man. "The man deserves to die," he had said, not realizing he was pronouncing his own death sentence. As we know, God, in His mercy, let King David live. David would see fulfilled, however, the second half of the judgment. "Four lambs for one," he had said. And tragically one after another, four of his sons met their doom.

As I studied the circumstances surrounding each death, I was reminded King David was not the one who killed Absalom; Absalom died in battle at the hand of Joab and his armor-bearers. Yet David felt guilty. This time, however, David's guilt, unlike the guilt he had experienced over his adultery with Bathsheba, would not lead to confession and restoration of his relationship with the Lord. In this case, there was nothing to confess and restore. Consequently, there could be no release.

"What I have suspected all along, Lord, has been confirmed in Your Word," I declared. "There are two kinds of guilt: one rooted in fact, the other related to feelings; one true, one false; one requiring confession, the other requiring action. You remove the first; we must remove the second."

I tried to translate all this into my life as a fractured Christian woman. I knew that at least some of my guilt was based in fact. By putting obligations before the Lord, I had broken the first commandment. I should feel guilty about this. The Lord promises, though, if we confess our sins, He will forgive us, removing all our guilt—a positive outcome for a bad situation. But I also recognized in my life the other kind of guilt: the harmful kind, the kind not based in fact. Whenever I would say,

"Sorry, I can't take on another thing!" I would feel guilty. If I even thought about saying that, guilt would come. I feared I would be judged by myself, others, the church, and God. Yet I would have done nothing wrong.

Confession doesn't work with this kind of guilt. This one takes action. We're required to do something. And the sooner, the better.

What Can We Do to Change Things?

Assess present obligations diligently: Do I enjoy doing this? Am I gifted for it? Does God want me to continue with it? When a desire, a talent, and a job match, there can be a special empowering of the Holy Spirit. Everyone ends up getting blessed: the giver, the receiver, and especially the Lord. When, however, desire and giftedness are absent, a ministry becomes mechanical. It can still be performed, but it won't have Holy Spirit power. So it makes sense to seek and to maintain a good "fit."

Carefully weigh any future involvement. Most opportunities to serve will be good ones. That makes it hard to choose. But choose we must: the best from the good. Otherwise, we will end up more fractured than we are now. Therefore, when weighing opportunities, it may help to ask:

- Which activities will bring God the most glory?
- Which will bring me the most joy?
- Who's pressuring me to choose this one?
- If I take it on, what will I have to sacrifice?
- How many jobs can I do efficiently?
- Have I sought advice?
- Have I prayed about my decision?

These questions should keep us from getting in over our heads.

Learn to say no. After all, our no may afford someone else the opportunity to say yes. Then two people will be blessed. However, whenever we refuse an obligation, especially one that is "Christian," we can expect guilt feelings to surface. It takes time before it's possible to say no without experiencing any guilt whatsoever.

Drop what needs to be dropped. To discontinue serving is a difficult decision, especially when we've been involved in a job for some time. "They need me," we think. And they do. But no human being is indispensable. We can all be replaced—and will be in time. So let's give God a little creative leeway. He may want to implement a solution we haven't even thought of. And it will be perfect.

Different people have different expectations concerning jobs. In some circles it's automatically assumed that when you sign up to do something, you sign up for life. That creates a problem for the volunteer who is thinking short term. How can she escape her life sentence gracefully, especially when she thinks she sees threats in the eyes of her jurors?

Compounding the problem are the perks. The longer we're in a job, the more we get used to its privileges. Some can be hard to give up. Pride taunts us. "See what you'll be missing?" it says. Whether we listen to pride or ignore it, one thing is sure: guilt will be there to take our hand. It can be a constant companion if we let it.

When we ask God to guide us, though, He will. He's more interested in our well-being than we are. Therefore, when we've made a prayerful decision, we can assume it's the correct one—at least until it proves to be otherwise. Even if we have misread God's direction, we have His promise to work all things for our good (see Rom. 8:28). So as Christians, we're safe to fail. Let's exercise this privilege freely.

Try not to second-guess decisions. Once a decision has been made, it's ancient history. We can't afford to think about what we would have done—or could have done—or should have done. It's imperative to put the past behind us and move forward in God's grace.

Be prepared to fight the enemy. His tactic is to get Christians so overextended they're not doing anything well. He does this by telling us we're shirking our duty if we say no—to anything! The guilt that results drives us until one day we break. Aha! A victory.

The enemy knows, though, we're too smart to get over-extended in activities that have no eternal value. So he tempts us with "church work." If we say no to something Christian, we feel guilty, really guilty. Then we become an easy target for manipulation. The only way to stop this degenerative sequence is to say, "Enough! No more! Period!"

Thankfully, as Christians we have victory in Jesus Christ. He went to the cross to remove our guilt. If He says it's gone, it's gone. We are now free. Let's learn to walk in that freedom: "Forgetting what is behind and straining toward what is ahead . . . press[ing] on toward the goal to win the prize for which God has called [us] heavenward in Christ Jesus" (Phil. 3:13–14).

Confirmation from God's Word

1. Read Luke 10:38–42 about Mary and Martha.
2. Ponder:
   - Since Martha is the one who welcomes Jesus when He arrives in town (v. 38), she obviously has an interest in sitting at Jesus' feet. Why doesn't she? (Note: If you read John 11:17–44 concerning the raising of Lazarus, you will see that Martha is the sister who goes to meet Jesus, while Mary stays home until summoned. Yet Martha is usually portrayed as the less spiritual one. Has she gotten a raw deal?)
   - Is there any indication Martha may feel resentful for having to work while her sister is learning (v. 40)?
   - If Mary were to help Martha in the kitchen, both could sit at Jesus' feet. Do you think Mary feels guilty for not helping? Should she?
   - Consider the activities of both women. Are both activities necessary? Good? How can it be said Mary has chosen the "better" activity (v. 42)? Is the "better" in one case necessarily the better in every case?
   - In what sense is Mary's choice permanent and "will not be taken away from her" (v. 42)? In what sense is Martha's choice "temporary"? Are there times when "temporary" choices are the correct ones? Why is this not such a time?

3. If you were to advise the FCW how to live for eternity in a world where routine chores have to be done—and to live without guilt—what would you tell her?

Part Three

How to
Restore Wholeness

here is a difference
between memorizing
Scripture and thinking Biblically . . .
knowing the words and experiencing their meaning . . .
having the sentences embedded in your head
and having their impact embedded in your heart . . .
believing that the words are right
and knowing they are true . . .
"doing Christianity" and being a Christian.
—Tim Hansel[8]

9

Word of God, Empower Me

"[My Word] will not return to me empty, but will accomplish
what I desire and achieve the purpose for which I sent it."
Isaiah 55:11

I turned the knob on the standing lamp near the sofa. No light. So I tried the lamp on the desk. It lit up immediately. "Well, we don't have a power failure," I concluded. "Maybe the sofa lamp just needs a new bulb."

I unscrewed the old bulb and went to the cupboard. Sixty watts. Sounds good. I twisted the new bulb into the socket and turned the knob a second time.

Nothing.

"I can't believe this!" I thought. "That lamp isn't old enough to have defective wiring."

"Lee," I shouted toward the den. "Something's wrong with the lamp by the sofa. Can you take a look at it?"

From the other room came a question: "Have you checked the plug?"

I was too embarrassed to answer. I had not checked the plug. In fact, the more I thought about it, the more I knew the plug was the problem. I had moved the sofa last evening to vacuum under it (something I don't do often), and I had moved the lamp in the process. I didn't even have to check. When I did, there it was: the culprit, lying close to its source of power but definitely not connected.

I felt stupid. Why had I missed the obvious? Why?

Listen to the Many Voices

* *The church*: "You must have a daily quiet time in the Word of God. It should take place first thing in the morning and last about an hour. You should look forward to it."

* *Christian friends*: "Devotional booklets are easy to read and take less time. Most of these combine Scripture verses with personal anecdotes, so you don't need to study the Bible itself."

* *Personal thoughts*: "You prepared your Sunday School lesson today; you don't need a devotional time."

* *The enemy*: "Drop your Bible reading altogether. You can invest your time more wisely by helping someone in need."

All voices in unison: "Listen to us; we're right."

Our response: "I can't sort it all out. Do I need a devotional time, or don't I? Can booklets and quarterlies be substitutes for the Word of God? Is ministry more important than study?"

A Lone Voice: "If you would listen to Me, you'd know. Everybody needs time in the Word, but how they get it can be individually tailored. So seek God's leading—moment by precious moment—and don't pay attention to other voices."

Accentuating the Positive

The small room in which the women's ministry committee was to meet that August evening was hot and stuffy. Trying to stay as cool as possible, most of us arrived in shorts, tank tops, and sandals. Thankfully, someone opened the windows, letting in a cool breeze.

The topic for discussion was "The Place of Scripture in the Lives of Busy Christian Women." I couldn't wait to hear what everybody had to say.

"Carol, why don't you start?" someone asked. After all,

Carol is the teacher of our women's Bible study.

"Okay," Carol agreed. "We all know the importance of food for the body. Well, food for the soul is just as important, even more so. But to get the most out of it, we have to eat regularly, balance our selections, and exercise the weight off. That's how to stay spiritually fit."

Carol is prepared, I thought. I was feeling guilty that I hadn't researched the topic more thoroughly.

"The Bible is God's refrigerator," Carol continued. "It holds everything Christians need for growth. There's milk for the young and meat for those who like to chew. There's also a variety of breads, vegetables, and fruit. There are even olives for those who like the exotic and fudge for people who want a special treat." (The chocoholics among us murmured longingly.)

When we collected ourselves, Sally said to Carol, "As you were talking, I thought how important it is for somebody like you to open the refrigerator door. Once I saw all that food, I couldn't wait to reach in. What a change! I used to pick up my Bible and force myself to read. Now I can hardly wait for my devotional time to come."

"I love reading the Bible, too," I interjected. "But I find myself in the minority. Most people use devotional booklets instead. What is your opinion of these?"

"I love them," Patti said, entering the discussion. "They're the 'fast food' of the Christian world. I don't know about the rest of you, but the faster the better for me."

Having watched Patti in action, we all chuckled knowingly. But underneath I found myself identifying with the hectic lifestyle that was driving her. And I admired the fact she had found a way to "eat" on the run.

"I'm glad I have a speaking ministry," I contributed. "That forces me to be in the Word of God. If I didn't have an obligation, I'm not sure I'd be faithful."

"Me either," Carol admitted. "But the amazing thing is that it doesn't matter what I'm preparing to do—teach the women's Bible study, lead a discussion, or give a talk—I get personally fed if I'm using the Bible."

"And you feed others," Sally continued. "Some Bible studies are dry, with no application to life. They make me feel like I'm wasting my time. Not so with yours."

"Actually, there's always an application," Carol countered, "if you listen with your own needs in mind. Disappointment comes when we depend too much on the teacher. If we depend on the Holy Spirit and are attentive to His voice, He'll touch our hearts every time—sometimes in powerful ways."

"I wish every woman could hear this discussion," I commented. "Some women are under such pressure to be in the Word 'properly' that they have developed a negative attitude toward the most positive Book of all. Do we have time to examine these pressures?"

"We can't afford not to," Carol agreed.

Overstatement and Truth

* *The FCW thinks*, "Even though I'm not a morning person, I must have my devotional time at the beginning of each day."

The Lone Voice whispers, "Bless the Lord at all times. Let His praise continually be in your mouth (see Ps. 34:1). Forcing yourself to have devotions at a time that isn't natural can result in a rush-through—'I've-got-to-get-it-done' attitude whereas reading the Word at a convenient time will make it a reward, a 'now-I'll-treat-myself' pleasure. Give God your best time, whenever it is, and He'll give you His choicest blessings."

* *The FCW thinks*, "I can't spend just a few minutes in the Word and expect to get blessed."

The Lone Voice whispers, "Why not? There's power in one thought alone: 'Peace!' In fact, a little of the Word assimilated is better than a lot merely tasted. So give it whatever time you can; then meditate on it the rest of the day."

* *The FCW thinks*, "If Bible verses don't leap out at me, I'm not spiritually tuned in."

The Lone Voice whispers, "Some seed lies dormant for a while before bursting into application. Let it."

* *The FCW thinks*, "If I don't feel like 'eating,' there's something wrong with me."

The Lone Voice whispers, "Eat anyway. It's your responsibility to feed yourself. It's God's responsibility to make the food taste good."

* *The FCW thinks*, "On days when my devotions get crowded

out, I feel like I'm letting God down."

The Lone Voice whispers, "There will be times when the 'tyranny of the urgent' takes over. God understands. Just snuggle into His arms and let Him refresh you with His Presence alone. He knows it's possible for you to skip a meal without starving to death. Just don't skip too many meals. Robust believers turn into spiritual anorexics this way."

* *The FCW thinks*, "Maybe I should switch to a devotional booklet. That will be faster than reading a couple of chapters from the Bible."

The Lone Voice whispers, "Careful! There is no substitute for the unfiltered Word of God. All Christians need at least some communication that comes firsthand. This doesn't mean you shouldn't use a devotional, but use it as a springboard for Bible reading rather than a replacement of it."

* *The FCW thinks*, "I like the days I prepare to teach my Sunday School class because then I don't need personal devotions."

The Lone Voice whispers, "Reading to give out and reading to take in are two different things. In addition to studying your Bible, read just for a blessing."

* *The FCW thinks*, "I am a doer. I don't have much time for Bible reading. I'd like to see how long I can go without it before my ministry runs dry."

The Lone Voice whispers, "Not long. A Christian who is not plugged into power cannot sustain an effective outreach."

A Divine Perspective

As a new believer I was fascinated with this book that claims to be the Word of God. So I decided to study it and let it speak for itself and about itself. What I learned astounded me. I had heard of money-back guarantees, even lifetime guarantees, but here was a book that came with an eternal guarantee, based upon its inherent life-changing capabilities. If I would faithfully tuck it into my heart, it would turn me into the woman I wanted to be. That was its promise!

As a former teacher of English, I had read and taught many books by a diversity of authors—even some I would like to forget—but never one with the power to produce a desired effect. Shakespeare was good at challenging me, but the Bible was promising to change me. What kind of changes would it make? I wondered. I was interested in specifics. So as I read, I listed specific claims. Here is what I found:

1. *The Bible will equip us fully for each and every task* (see 2 Tim. 3:16). It will teach us correct beliefs, rebuke us when we waver, correct us when we take the wrong path, and train us in righteous living, I learned.

That sounds like everything I need to care for my world, I concluded. Let me at it!

2. *The Bible shows us what's inside us* (see Heb. 4:12). It "penetrates" our souls and spirits, I read, and "judges" our thoughts and attitudes.

"Hold on there! I'm not sure I like having God take an x-ray of my innards," I exclaimed. The woman who wants to make correct decisions, though, has to examine her heart's motivations, I was guessing. She can't take the Bible's attractive characteristics without taking the distasteful too, especially if they're all for her good. So I decided to make regular visits to the spiritual radiology department and to take the Doctor's report of my condition seriously, even if I didn't like it.

3. *Reading the Bible can increase our faith*. "Faith comes by hearing the message, and the message is heard through the Word of Christ," I noted (Rom. 10:17). How wonderful, I thought, to have a place to get spiritually recharged. I liked this promise.

4. *The Bible illuminates the road before us, guiding us through life's highway system*. "Your Word is a lamp to my feet and a light for my path," it says of itself (Ps. 119:105). As I read this promise, I figured the "lamp" was probably more like a lantern than a searchlight. It would show me where I was, not where I'd eventually be. The journey's overview would be saved for heaven. There we'd be privileged to lay out the map, hold up the lantern, and marvel at the complexity of the plan. What a joy to see the intersection of roads and why they met where they did! For now, though, I knew I was called to trust the Mapmaker and to keep on walking. "Lord, take my hand," I found myself praying. He did.

5. *The Bible cleanses us from dirt we pick up along life's journey* (see Eph. 5:26). As it washes away impurities, it brings refreshment to the soul. There's one catch, though: it's up to us to turn on the water. Otherwise, there will be no shower of blessings.

"Don't let me go to bed dirty," I prayed, "either outside or in."

6. *The Bible can keep us from sinning* (see Ps. 19:11). However to receive this benefit, we have to hide it in our hearts, we're told. As I contemplated the challenge of Bible memorization, I hesitated. I don't memorize easily. But I wanted a divine restraint on my activities, one that would warn me, "No further, Peg." So I decided to read selected verses over and over, until they became part of me. I use the same method of memorization today. And it still checks my wanderings. It can do the same for children who hide the Word in their hearts. What an incentive to encourage our kids to participate in a Bible memory program!

7. *The Bible comforts us in suffering—by "preserving" us and giving us hope, it says* (see Ps. 119:49–50). It's nice to know the same Scripture that encouraged saints years ago has the power to encourage me today, I thought. I can receive a word from the Lord any time of the day or night just by opening my Bible. That thrilled me. It still does.

8. *The Bible can transform us into the likeness of Christ* (see 2 Cor. 3:18). It does this, it claims, through the power of the Holy Spirit, who is not only the Author of the Word but its Enabler as well. When we hold up the "mirror" (identified in Jas. 1:23 as God's Word), we see two images: Christ in His perfection and ourselves in our imperfection. If we focus on ourselves, we get depressed. If, however, we focus on Christ and continue to do so, eventually His image will superimpose itself on ours and we will become like Him!

How's that for motivation? Why, if my bathroom mirror had the ability to make me what I want to be, I'd be gazing into it day and night. Oh well, one out of two isn't bad, I decided, especially when the "one" makes changes that are eternal.

When I finished my search for effectual promises, I traced verbs, action words indicating built-in capability. The following is a partial listing of what I found. The Bible promises to:

activate	convict	equip	rebuke	strengthen
challenge	convince	feed	refresh	teach
change	correct	guide	renew	train
charge	empower	instruct	restore	
cleanse	energize	motivate	restrain	
comfort	enlighten	preserve	revitalize	

Once I had this list alphabetized, I stopped to ask myself, "Can I afford to skip any of these blessings?" Every day I will face a choice. Will I let 'the worries of this life, the deceitfulness of wealth, and the desire for other things crowd out my devotional time (see Matt. 13:22)? Or will I be faithful to read a portion of God's Word each day, then meditate on what I've read until the Word takes root and bears fruit in my life?"

The enemy would be after me, I knew. He will do anything to keep a believer and the Bible apart. But I also knew I had the wherewithal to defeat him. My strategy would be an initial resolve not to go to bed until I'd read the Bible. This would be followed up with periodic checkups and reminders.

Now, many years later, my resolve is still intact and my periodic checkups and reminders still necessary. But oh, how blessed I have been! I have tried every promise and found it true. "Continue to keep me faithful, Lord," I pray. "I want Your power to be evident within me every day."

What Can We Do to Change Things?

Block out time for a daily appointment with God in His Word. If we don't schedule it, it may not take place. But if it's on the calendar, it will, for women are diligent about honoring their appointments. This particular appointment is to read Scriptures in a version that is easy to understand. If preferred, the reading may be combined with or incorporated in a devotional booklet. But let's remember that the power to change us lies in the Bible itself—and only there.

When we read the Word, it is common to experience frustration. Some Scriptures are difficult to understand. It goes over our heads. No problem. It's our job to feed the data into our computers; it's God job to do the processing. Other Scripture stays in the computer's memory for years before it is retrieved. Again, no problem. God is responsible for making application; we are responsible for absorbing information. What doesn't apply to our lives may be designed for somebody's else's life. We don't have to understand or find an application for every verse we come upon.

Knowing this, we can approach our appointment with God expectantly, for He speaks personally through His Word. However, to have a personal encounter, it helps to meet God's prerequisites:

"In the desert prepare the way for the Lord; make straight in the wilderness a highway for our God . . . And the glory of the Lord will be revealed" (Isa.40:3–5).

As we part our mounds of daily concerns and create an uncluttered pathway, God will meet us, I believe, the same way He met John the Baptist when he prepared the way (see John 1:23). God's Holy Spirit will stand before us, offering refreshment to our souls. Then in time He will speak, and what He says will be enlightening. We will see God's glory revealed in a way that meets the day's every need. What a beautiful promise!

To hear God speak in a world of noise, however, can be a challenge. So let me offer two suggestions. First, before opening the Word, ask the Lord to speak to you. Second, while reading the Word, listen for His message. It's important to listen not with the intellect only but with the heart as well. Occasionally, God's reward will be dramatic. A phrase from the Bible will swell into two-foot high letters, leap off the page, and establish itself forever in our lives. Dramatic or not, however, God always speaks through His Word. "This is my message for you today," He says.

"I receive it," we reply. We know then that we have prepared a highway, and our God has met us on it.

Have personal devotions when we're wide awake and can expect a minimum of distractions. A day consists of twenty-four hours, regardless of when the counting starts. Beginning the day with Scripture gets us off to a good start, but it's not a biblical mandate to have devotions first thing in the morning. We are free to choose a time when our receptivity is at its peak. This could be early morning (before everyone else is up), late at night (when everyone else is in bed), or any time in between. God is more readily available than we are—and much more accessible. In fact, He's waiting for us to make our appointment—and then to keep it.

Set a realistic time limit to our devotions. It's better to ask, "Is our meeting over already?" than to check our watches and groan, "I have to do this ten more minutes." Cut it short and feel guilty or keep going and get nothing out of it—what a choice! This is a meeting with God! Let's keep it short enough to be as exhilarating as it is meant to be. The time can always be extended. But let's be careful: it's sweet to leave ourselves wanting more.

Meet with God at the same time and in the same place each day.

A great portion of the Christian life consists of discipline and habit. The object, in this case, is to establish a habit that is good—one that becomes so ingrained in our routine that when we miss it, we really miss it! It is true that absence can make the heart grow fonder, but absence can also be the beginning of a bad habit. As every farmer will tell us, ruts are hard to get out of. Since life consists of lots of them, it makes sense to pick our ruts carefully. Chances are that we'll be in them a long, long time.

Once we've established our meeting time, we can choose our place. We may select the kitchen table, a chair in the family room, or a desk in a bedroom. The place doesn't matter, but the "setting apart" of the place does. "At this time each day, Lord, I will do nothing in this spot except read Your Word." Hopefully, this dedication ceremony will make it difficult to doze or daydream, for we have established that we are coming to this spot for a very important purpose!

Finding the right spot can be a challenge though. One woman sits in a chair facing the corner of her bedroom, then pictures God in the spot where the walls meet. Another retreats to the bathroom, the only place she's assured of privacy. Even there she gets interrupted, she says. Still another puts a towel over her head when she's at her kitchen sink. She can mentally block out what's happening around her, she reports. When I expressed concern for her preschoolers, she said, "Don't worry. God protects them while I'm 'gone.' Besides, I can 'come back' quickly if necessary."

We may have to try several techniques before we find one that works. But experimentation can be fun.

Incorporate God's Word into our daily routines. Then when we're forced to miss a devotional time, we're still "plugged in." Here are some suggestions I have used:

1. Place Scripture verses in strategic spots—on the bathroom mirror, by the stove, and on the car's visor. Review them regularly: while grooming, cooking, driving, etc.

2. During impossibly busy times, hold spontaneous momentary "church" services in the "sanctuary" of my heart.

3. During "breaks," meditate on Scriptures that need to be worked into my life: "What does this mean, Lord? Does it have an application now?"

4. Ask God to use the Scripture to guide me as I make

decisions.

    5. Use God's Word as a straight edge:

        a. To show compliance or deviation in my own
           thinking

        b. To show compliance or deviation in the voices I am
           hearing, even those that seem to come from God.

God's Word is a power-house of blessing. I, for one, don't want to miss out on anything that has my name on it. "So keep me true to my own desires, Lord. I really want to become like You."

Confirmation from God's Word

Note: Many Christians find it helpful to mark their Bibles. However, if you feel it is wrong to do this, complete the following exercises mentally:

    1. Read Psalm 119 describing the power of Scripture.

    2. Note the power of the Word to *preserve* (also translated "quicken, revive, refresh, renew, restore, give back life again"). You should find this concept in eleven verses (vv. 25, 37, 40, 50, 88, 93, 107, 149, 154, 156, 159). In what kinds of situations will the Word "preserve" us?

    3. Notice the synonyms for Scripture: Word, testimonies, ways, precepts, law, statutes, decrees, commandments, judgments, ordinances, and promises. Highlight these synonyms. (You should have highlighted words in all verses except five: vv. 84, 90, 121, 122, and 132).

    4. Now circle the parts of the human body which are mentioned or implied (heart, mind, eyes, ears, mouth, hands, and feet).

    5. Note the relationship of the Word of God to each of these body parts ("hide it in the heart," v. 11; "meditate" on it with the mind, v. 15, etc.).

    6. If the FCW were to integrate the Word of God into every aspect of her being—from the top of her head to the tip of her toes—in what ways would she begin functioning as a "whole" person, rather than as a fragmented one?

In prayer you align yourself
to the purposes
and power of God, and He is able to do things
that through you He couldn't otherwise do.
—E. Stanley Jones, missionary statesman

10

Father, Teach Me to Pray

Pray continually; give thanks in all circumstances,
for this is God's will for you in Christ Jesus.
1 Thessalonians 5:17–18

"Mary and Grace are rooming together at a Christian convention like this one," the speaker began. "Both want to please God with their lives. After a full day of meetings, they retire to their hotel room.

"Once they have showered and snuggled into their robes, they flop onto their respective beds and discuss the lectures they have heard. When they feel they are all talked out, they say good-night and turn out the light.

"At this point, Mary kneels by her bed and starts to pray. For about forty-five minutes she pours out her heart to God, interceding for her family, her friends, her church, her neighbors, her coworkers and missionaries stationed around the world. When she has finished mentioning everything she can think of, she rises slowly to her feet and falls into bed, exhausted.

"Grace merely says, 'Good-night, Lord,' and slips beneath the covers.

"Now I have a question for you," the speaker interjected. "Which woman has the more vital connection to God?"

I shifted in my chair in the vast convention hall. My answer came easily. "Mary, of course! But if that's the answer, why the question?"

"This is not an easy question to answer," the speaker continued, as if reading my thoughts. "It is natural to think the woman who prays the longest and hardest has the most vital link to the Lord. But I'm not sure this is so. There may be more to this subject of prayer than is apparent."

Indeed there is.

Listen to the Many Voices

* "Pray long and hard, mentioning every need you can think of."

* "Don't stop praying until you get an answer."

* "Once you've prayed about something, you don't need to pray again. God has heard."

* "Don't pray while doing anything else. Save prayer for private times, when you can concentrate."

* "Kneel, bow your head, clasp your hands, and shut your eyes. Show respect to the King of kings."

* "Learn to use 'thee's' and 'thou's.' Address God reverently."

* "Learn to pray Scripture. It never returns void."

* "Repeat the Lord's Prayer. It's divinely approved."

* "God wants to hear you when you pray, so be audible."

All voices in unison: "If you are a Christian who means business with God, you will learn how to pray."

Our response: "My prayer life is a disaster. I don't have time to pray during the day. And by the time night comes, I'm too tired. Yet I want to have meaningful communion with God. What can I do?"

A Lone Voice: "In the cacophony of sounds around you, learn how to listen to Me. That will be the beginning of a successful prayer life."

Accentuating the Positive

As our adult Sunday School class was letting out, I positioned myself outside the door. I was hoping to catch Miss Knowles, an elderly saint known for marvelous answers to her prayers.

"What's the secret to learning how to pray?" I blurted as she came within hearing distance.

"Doing it—just doing it," Miss Knowles smiled. I leaned closer as folks passed by.

"The first thing you have to do," she continued, "is to set aside a time to do nothing but pray. Let God speak through His Word, then respond—in one beautiful act of worship. But it's important to plan the event. That way it's more likely to occur."

By this time the Sunday School room had cleared of people, so Miss Knowles and I stepped back inside. As I arranged two chairs, I said, "I hope I'm not keeping you."

"Certainly not," this pillar of our church replied. "There's nothing I'd rather talk about than prayer."

"Great," I said enthusiastically. "I've got a couple more questions. "Number one, how familiar can you be with God?"

"God is holy," this wise woman answered with a hush. "He should be approached with awe. And although in Jesus Christ God became personal, considering Him a 'buddy,' as some young people do these days, is simply not appropriate. We must remember we're entering the presence of the King of kings."

"Does that mean we have to be on our knees with our heads bowed, hands clasped, and eyes shut?" I pressed, thinking of the relatively few times I had prayed precisely that way.

"No, but such a posture does show respect," she replied. "Besides, the image you just described is a recognized posture of prayer. When you see somebody kneeling, you assume prayer is taking place, don't you?"

"Yes, I do. But now to question number two. How does a beginner learn to pray?"

"Well," Miss Knowles began, her eyes lighting up, "how does a child learn to talk?"

"By repeating what his parents say," I answered.

"Exactly," she affirmed. "The disciples learned to pray by following the example Jesus gave them in 'The Lord's Prayer.' So can you."

"Does this mean I have to recite those very words?"

"Of course not," Miss Knowles answered gently. "But the way that particular prayer is constructed makes it a good model to follow.

"However, there are other prayers that bear repeating, too," she claimed as she opened her Bible. "For example, I start each day with 'Yours, O Lord, is the greatness and the power and the glory and the majesty and the splendor.' from King David's prayer in 1 Chronicles 29. That gives me a positive mind-set." I jotted down the reference.

"Before reading the Bible, I pray, 'Search me, O God, and know my heart' from Psalm 139. That makes me receptive to God's message." By now Miss Knowles was leafing from Scripture to Scripture.

"After committing a sin, I plead, 'Have mercy upon me, O God' from Psalm 51. I need to be cleansed."

This saint paused a moment, then she continued, "And if I want to pray for a friend, I just recite Philippians 1:9–11, inserting my friend's name in the appropriate places. I can't think of any better way to pray than to ask that 'love may abound more and more in knowledge and depth of insight.' I pray the same prayer for myself, concentrating on the 'pure and blameless' part." With this she chuckled.

But as she put her Bible down, I noticed tears in her eyes. Then she asked, "Is it possible to express human feelings more beautifully than this? If mere earthlings enjoy such sentiments, imagine the Lord's joy when His children use words they learned at His knee."

By this time I found myself longing for a vibrant prayer life.

"One more question, Miss Knowles," I begged. "Could you comment on audible versus inaudible prayers?"

"It is good to pray aloud," she encouraged. "When words are actually spoken, a distinction is made between what is merely a thought and what one wants to express." My mentor was glancing at her watch.

"I can't tell you how much I appreciate your sharing your wisdom, Miss Knowles," I told her gratefully. "But we'd better get into the sanctuary or we'll miss the opening hymn. Would it be possible for us to meet again? I want to sort out some misconceptions about prayer—misconceptions that are fracturing the modern Christian woman."

"It would be a privilege to talk with you—and to contribute to that book you're writing," she assured me, placing her hand on my arm. "How about tomorrow night at 8:00?"

I agreed. What follows is what came from that meeting on prayer:

Overstatement and Truth

* *The FCW thinks*, "God doesn't hear 'on-the-run' prayers. I'd better go to my 'prayer closet.'"

The Lone Voice whispers, "God hears all prayers no matter where or when they are uttered."

* *The FCW thinks*, "I've got to keep praying until I get an answer."

The Lone Voice whispers, "In some situations one prayer is sufficient. In others, God wants you to persist. The more sensitive you are to God's voice, the easier it will be to know when you've 'prayed through.'"

* *The FCW thinks*, "The woman who kneels and shuts her eyes is more spiritual than the one who prays in motion."

The Lone Voice whispers, "There are many biblically approved postures for prayer. Abraham's servant bowed down; Joshua fell on his face; David sat; Solomon stood, spreading his hands; and Jesus knelt, looking toward heaven. So pray in a way that fits the situation. But a word of caution: if you pray while driving, keep your eyes open and remain in an upright position."

* *The FCW thinks*, "The people I consider super spiritual use the King James English in their prayers."

The Lone Voice whispers, "God is less interested in how you talk than in that you talk. Just tell Him what's on your heart."

* *The FCW thinks*, "It's up to me to initiate communication with God."

The Lone Voice whispers, "Where did you get that idea? Prayer is response. The communication that sets it in motion begins in heaven. Long before you even think of asking, God is preparing His answer (see Isa. 65:24). But you must ask."

A Divine Perspective

One day, several years ago, as I was reading the charge Moses gave to God's people in Deuteronomy 30, I came upon these words, "Love the Lord your God, listen to his voice, and hold fast to him" (v. 20). As I evaluated these three commands and my own response to them, my score was low. I needed to work on listening.

But how can we hear God speak, I wondered, in this age of hi-tech sound? We're bombarded with noise: the drone of the TV, the shriek of the hair dryer, the moan of the dishwasher, the rumble of traffic, the buzz of the computer printer, and the screams of jet planes. How in the world are we supposed to hear God?

Hoping for an answer, I decided to search the Bible for ways God claims to speak. Then I could respond, and my response would be "prayer." Here is what I found:

1. God speaks through nature. "The heavens declare the glory of God" (see Ps. 19:1–4). The night "whispers" and the days "pour forth" evidence a Creator exists:

- The stars proclaim, "God made us."
- The flowers plead, "Examine our design."
- The seasons state, "God brings life out of death."

In fact, the message of creation is so powerful, it is hard to ignore it. Yet only the believer really "hears" and, in turn, is prompted to respond, "My God, how great You are!" When this response occurs, it is prayer.

2. God speaks through the conscience. "Don't do it!" or "Do do it!" (see Rom. 2:15). Our reaction to this advice is mixed. We either ignore it or are grateful for it. When we say, "Thank You, Lord, for caring enough to guide me," our gratitude becomes a prayer.

3. God speaks through the Bible. "Herein lies power to change your life," the Word of God proclaims. "Will you let it happen?"

Actually, of all the ways God speaks, the Bible is the *only* way that is 100 percent reliable. The Scripture calls itself "a more certain Word"—a Word through which all other messages must be filtered to see if their origin is divine (see 2 Peter 1:19–21). They are the only voice that needs no testing. They are inspired, infallible, and authoritative—our only rule for faith and practice.

"Thank You, Lord, for giving me a standard by which to measure the many conflicting voices in my life," we say. When this thanksgiving pours out, we are praying.

4. God speaks through people. "In the past, God spoke to our forefathers through the prophets (Heb. 1:1). But does God have prophets today?" we ask.

Well, in a sense, anyone who proclaims God's Word is a prophet, but unlike the prophets quoted in the Bible, our contemporaries are not infallible. This does not mean, however, we shouldn't listen to what they are saying.

"Let's visit the nursing home today," a friend suggests.

"Maybe we should," we think. "Maybe my friend is God's agent, designated to 'spur [me] on toward love and good deeds' (see Heb. 10:24). "After all, God does command us to "be kind and compassionate to one another" (Eph. 4:32).

"Okay," we respond. "Let's go!" When we declare these intentions to God, we are praying.

5. God speaks through a "still small voice." "This is how I want you to apply Scripture to your life," the Spirit may whisper as He confirms suggestions that come through other voices. Unlike the rest, however, this voice is "direct," coming from deep within the soul.

In the course of a day, many thoughts, feelings, and impressions impact us with their messages. Most are not of divine origin. How do we sort out which are?

Well, let me share my own series of tests. If an idea is:

- personally convicting (I have no rest until I do it)
- God-glorifying (perhaps at the expense of my own glory)
- others-benefitting (an idea I would not have thought of myself) and
- supported by Scripture (it lies within the realm of what a Christian should do), the idea is almost certainly from God.

A lamb that has become accustomed to its Shepherd's voice recognizes it, the Bible says (see John 10:3), even if it's a "gentle whisper" (see 1 Kings 19:12). In fact, God's sheep "will never follow a stranger; . . . they will run away from him because they do not recognize a stranger's voice" (John 10:5). When we acquiesce to the Shepherd's urging by saying, "I'll go where you want me to go and do what you want me to do," this is prayer.

By the time I finished this study, I was so excited I couldn't wait to start "listening." Now, many years later, I have little trouble recognizing God's voice. My challenge now is obeying. So my current prayer is this: "Lord, get me to the place where I stop fighting You, where I do what You say, period."

Will that place ever come? I wonder.

What Can We Do to Change Things?

Study biblical prayers as models. Let me share several prayers that have inspired me.

I read Psalm 32, where King David prayed and his sins were forgiven. Then I myself pray, "Lord, I am a sinner, too. Please have mercy on Me."

I read 1 Kings 18:16–46, where the prophet Elijah prayed and two miracles occurred: fire descended from heaven and rain refreshed a thirsty land. Then I myself pray, "Father, demonstrate through me the same kind of power you demonstrated through Elijah, for I am feeling weak today."

I read Judges 6 and 7, where Gideon prayed and defeated an entire army with only a handful of men. Then I myself pray, "Lord, I feel as if I'm losing ground. I need affirmation as marvelous as Gideon's."

I read Exodus 32, where Moses prayed and God spared a nation from destruction. Then I myself pray, "Father, save our nation, too. It's playing fast and loose with Your principles."

I read Genesis 18:1–15 and 21:1–7, where Abraham prayed and fathered a child when he was one hundred years old. (His wife Sarah was ninety.) Then I myself pray, "Lord, I love reading this account of postmenopausal childbirth, but don't repeat this miracle, pleeeease!"

As I contemplate these incredible answers to prayer, I am heartened by the fact that these were ordinary people, struggling with the stress of everyday life. Sometimes they buckled under. David, I remembered, committed adultery; Elijah suffered from depression; Gideon questioned God's word; Moses lashed out in anger; Abraham lied to protect himself; and Sarah laughed at God's promise. In spite of their failings, however, they all had one thing going for them: they believed in an extraordinary God and knew how to tap His power through prayer.

Learn to "practice the presence of God." This refreshing concept was introduced to me by Brother Lawrence, a lame monk working in a monastery kitchen. He said, "For me the time of action does not differ from the time of prayer, and in the noise and clatter of my kitchen, while several persons are calling for as many different things, I possess God in as great tranquility as when upon my knees."[9]

As I read these words, I felt our brother had probably become ensnared at one time or another in the trap of compartmentalization (time for work, time for prayer) and had realized this was not the way the Christian life was supposed to be. In desperation, he learned the secret of integration (incorporating the sacred with the secular), thereby "sanctifying" everything he did. "O Lord," I found myself praying, "teach me the same life-changing lesson."

"Pray continually," the Bible commands (1 Thess. 5:17). Surely, this is not suggesting a constantly repeated litany of petitions, as we are apt to call our prayers. Rather, it refers to prayer without an "s," which is more of a mind-set, a receptive approach to life around us, a consuming consciousness that God is. Then, from a heart that's aware of who is making it beat comes a response. The awareness, the response, the whole process: this is prayer.

Oh, to have communion with the Creator that is so natural it's like breathing! Inhaling His presence and exhaling our awe. Then we won't have to worry about whether we make it to our prayer closets or not. We will know what it means to be praying all the time!

Offer songs of praise to the Lord, especially while doing chores. There are some wonderful prayers set to music. In fact, it's possible to sing praises to each Person of the Trinity individually. For example,

- "Father I Adore Thee"
- "My Jesus, I Love Thee"
- "Spirit of the Living God, Fall Fresh on Me."

The Bible urges, "Sing and make music in your heart to the Lord" (Eph. 5:19). Not only is this advice therapeutic, but in practice it is contagious. It's an easy way to create a joyful atmosphere in the home.

Practice shooting "prayer darts" to heaven. These are short statements that take no more than a moment to formulate, yet they do the job. For example,

1. When rising: "Good morning, Your Majesty."
2. While grooming: "I want to glorify You in my body, Lord."
3. When sending my family off: "Father, keep them safe."
4. When starting the car: "Protect me, Lord— and everyone who comes in my path."
5. When arriving at work: "Lord, make me a testimony of

your righteousness."

6. When going to a church meeting: "Lord, make me an instrument of your peace."
7. When needing wisdom: "Guide me, Father."
8. When facing a crisis: "Take over, Lord."
9. After committing a sin: "Forgive me, Lord."
10. After receiving a blessing: "Thank You, Lord."
11. For no reason at all: "I love You, Lord."
12. Before retiring: "Good night, Father." (That's all that's necessary. We will have been communicating all day).

Set aside a time reserved exclusively for prayer. Strive to honor it each day. Choose a setting with as little distraction as possible. "When you pray," the Bible advises, "go into your room [and] close the door" (Matt. 6:6).

This prayer time can come at the end of our devotional Bible reading or be altogether separate. Our prayers are more apt to be God-approved, however, if we let the Father speak to us before we speak to Him. When we spend time in God's Word, His will becomes impressed on our hearts. By the time we get around to offering our petitions, we don't have to ask, "Am I praying in the will of God?" We already know we are. We're merely verbalizing a burden He has already placed upon us.

It's as if God is saying, "I had planned to give you that anyway, but I was waiting until you asked." John the apostle puts it this way: "This is the assurance we have in approaching God: that if we ask anything according to his will, he hears us. And if we know that he hears us—whatever we ask—we know that we have what we asked of him" (1 John 5:14–15). Is there a more exciting Scripture anywhere?

In addition to praying alone, it is a good idea to set aside a time each week to pray with a friend. For fourteen years I met with my friend Judy to pray on behalf of our families. Over the years we watched our kids weather the trials of grade school, junior high, high school, college, career, engagement, marriage, and now parenting. As we look at some of the pitfalls that could have ensnared them—pitfalls that did ensnare some of their friends—we can only praise our Lord, who chose to honor our heartfelt pleas. Though Judy and I are now miles apart, we still bring the needs of our families to the Lord. We consider it a precious privilege.

Corporate prayer, with members of the body of Christ, is also beneficial. To offer praises and petitions as a group and to watch the answers come—what a boost to faith! When we consider the analysis of snow, we get some idea of the power of corporate bonding. Each flake alone must feel quite inconsequential in the huge scheme of things. But united with other flakes, it can cause entire cities to reconsider their plans. Regular corporate prayer is powerful stuff!

But should we have to miss our appointed time to talk with God, it's not as if we've lost our salvation. There's no Prayer Monitor in the Sky, checking attendance. God does, however, look forward to having us talk to Him. "Let me hear your voice," He says, "for your voice is sweet" (Song of Songs 2:14). When we consider the empty feeling we get when we haven't heard from a loved one for a while, we appreciate how God must feel when He doesn't hear from us. In this case, though, we can rectify the situation!

Use the same prayer format each day. Then if interrupted, it's easy to pick up where we left off. A prayer order often suggested spells ACTS:

1. A doration of God
2. C onfession of sins
3. T hanksgiving for blessings
4. S upplication (for ourselves, our husbands, kids, parents, relatives, friends, church, community, country, and our world).

This order reminds me of a character in the Pulitzer Prize-winning play *Our Town*, by Thornton Wilder, who addressed a letter as follows: "Grovers Corner, New Hampshire, United States of America, North America, Earth, Solar System, Milky Way Galaxy, the Universe, the Mind of God." I love it!

For me, it helps to picture the people I want to pray for standing in a series of concentric circles. I am positioned in the center, so I pray for myself first. My family, in order of age, is in the circle next to mine. Distant relatives with their "distant" concerns are positioned in a circle farther out. So it goes. This order helps me not only to pray first and foremost for loved ones closest to me, but also to continue praying at the right spot when interruptions come. And they do come.

Break down barriers to effectual prayer. "The prayer of a righteous man is powerful and effective," the Bible tells us (Jas. 5:16), but there are things that can hinder a prayer's effectiveness. For example,

- Disobeying God's commands (Deut. 1:43–46)
- Harboring unconfessed sin (Ps. 66:18)
- Having a stingy spirit (Prov. 21:13)
- Promoting selfish desires (Jas. 4:3)
- Having an unforgiving heart (Mark 11:25)
- Failing to respect one's spouse (1 Pet. 3:7)

(This last barrier is addressed to husbands.)

Hopefully, at the first sign a wall is being erected, we'll be armed and ready to knock it down. We don't want anything to come between us and our Lord.

There is another hindrance to prayer, however, that may be even more of a threat to the fractured Christian woman: her own wandering thoughts. It's possible for a prayer session that starts out with pure intentions to end up something like this:

"Thank You, Lord, for such a nice, warm, sunny day. . . . Golly, I hear the kids playing ball. What if they trample the flowers? Watch out for the shrubbery, kids!

"Sorry for the interruption, Father. Now, back to my prayers. Thank You for my husband, Lee. . . . Gee, I wonder if he'll remember to pick up milk on his way home from work. No cereal tomorrow if he doesn't.

"Uh oh, I blew it again, Lord. Let me try one more time. Thank You for my kids. You know how much I love them. . . . Oh brother, their music lessons are today. I wonder if they've practiced enough.

"I sure hope Your love is still unconditional, Father, because I can't seem to keep my mind on what I'm doing. If it's okay with You, I'll have another go at it. Lord, I appreciate the sweet fellowship You've given me with each of my friends. . . . Hey, I wonder if Cheryl found that blouse she was looking for to match her new suit.

"I can't believe this, God! I'm really ashamed of myself. Now, back to my concentric circles. And, please, help me to concentrate. I want to thank You for our pastor. He faithfully preaches Your Word. . . . Gosh, I wonder if he'll try to squeeze another sermon out of the Book of Jonah. I feel like I'm the one in the belly of that fish. Let me out!

"There I go again! At least I'm almost to the end of my prayer list. God, please bless Your missionaries. I don't have time to mention their countries, but You already know where they are. . . Boy, it sure would be nice to visit Kenya this summer. All those exotic animals within camera range! We do have frequent flier miles. Maybe. . . .

"Forgive me, Lord, I've been distracted too many times today. I'll try to do better tomorrow. . . ." I wonder, though, if I will.

Chances are, I will not. Why do we think talking to God in a place designated only for prayer (our prayer closet) will solve the problem of distraction? We bring our own random thought process with us, no matter where we go. While it does help to be in a quiet place, we still have to control our mental wanderings. In fact, I'm learning that praying in a scheduled spot is no easier for me than communicating with God in the marketplace, on the road, or standing at the sink. Wherever I am, I have to make an effort to block out intrusions and to concentrate, focusing on the task at hand.

Toss cares, like tennis balls, to the Lord. "Cast all your anxiety on him because he cares for you," the Bible says (1 Pet. 5:7). This involves taking every single concern about any one situation, I believe, and verbalizing it to God. When we are finished, we discover that our voices have served as vehicles through which our anxieties have exited. Frankly, I'm glad I have a voice!

The trouble with tossing tennis balls to the Lord, though, is that sometimes they bounce back. In that case, we just have to toss them again and keep tossing until those balls stay put.

Pray naturally, as friend conversing with friend. Although when we pray, God delights in hearing words of His own composition and stops short of condemning repetition, He does condemn vain repetition, the "babblings of pagans"—words that have become meaningless through repeated renderings (see Matt. 6:7).

It is possible for even mature Christians to fall into a repetition trap. Although we may not repeat the Lord's Prayer endlessly, we do repeat phrases like "Praise the Lord!" or "Thank You, Jesus" over and over again, causing the listener to wonder if we're aware of what we are saying.

It is comforting to know, though, that God hears prayers no matter how they are phrased. In fact, the prayers of new believers (before they have been exposed to Christian jargon) can be precious. You won't hear, "Grant us journeying mercies" or "Extend Your watch-care over us, Lord" because new believers aren't used to talking like that. When we allow them to express themselves naturally, their prayers can be quite refreshing.

The director of a Christian mission which rehabilitates alcoholics tells the story of a habitual drunkard who had recently come to Christ and was now a member of a musical band sponsored by the mission. At his first prayer meeting, the director instructed him to "talk to God as if He were a friend, sitting next to you."

So that's what the convert did. He began his prayer by thanking the Lord for forgiving the sins of his past. These he enumerated in graphic detail. "But something is crazy, God," he blurted, "all I do now is play this ____ drum."

And with that, every seasoned Christian in the room smiled. Perhaps the Father in heaven did, too.

Confirmation from God's Word

1. Read 1 Chronicles 29:10–22 regarding King David's thanksgiving.

2. Ponder:
  • Does David follow the acrostic ACTS, or is his prayer more "integrated"?
  Find expressions of:
  • Adoration
  • Personal and corporate unworthiness
  • Thanksgiving
  • Supplication.
  Using your own prayer pattern as a standard, can you explain why David prays in the particular order he does?
  • What attributes of God does David acknowledge (vv. 10–13)?
  • For what does he express thanks (vv. 14–17)?
  • What petitions does he offer (vv. 18–19)?
  • What posture of prayer do the people employ (v. 20)? Why this, do you suppose?
  • Do you see any connection between the joy the people experience the next day (v. 22) and their praises to God a few hours before (v. 20)?

3. If the FCW were to recite verses 10 through 13 every morning, what effect would it have on her attitude toward her daily routine? On her relationship with her family? On her job performance? On the way she conducts her ministries? Why?

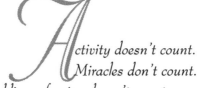

ctivity doesn't count.
Miracles don't count.
Public profession doesn't count.
Converts don't count. And good works don't count.
They are all nothing but leaves.
Only one thing counts in discerning a Christian from
a non-Christian: the fruit of his life before God and man.
—Peg Rankin[10]

11

Make Me Like You, Lord Jesus

For those God foreknew he also predestined
to be conformed to the likeness of his son.
Romans 8:29

"**O**h, no!" I cried as I gazed out the kitchen window of my home in Michigan. "It's going to be a bumper crop."

The land on which our house had been built used to be an orchard, and thirty fruit trees were left standing. Unaware their function had changed, those trees were continuing to do what they had always done: produce fruit.

Autumn was coming, and the fruit was ripening fast. Each tree had the potential of yielding several hundred pears, and I had a strong sense of stewardship.

"What am I going to do with the pears this year?" I wondered. "I've made pear sauce, pear crunch, pear pie, pear jam, and pear muffins. I've canned pears, frozen pears, and dried pears. I've raked pears and used them for fertilizer. I've given pears to my friends and left some on the doorsteps of my enemies. I've even advertised pears at ridiculous prices and let bargain hunters swarm all over the place."

"Stop producing! Stop producing!" I barked through the open window.

There was no response. Fruit trees are programmed to produce. They don't think about it, plan for it, or work at it. They just do it. Their fruit is an extension of their nature.

"Why isn't mine?" I wondered.

Listen to the Many Voices

* "Christians are known by their fruit. So produce."
* "A fruit of the Spirit is faithfulness" (Translation: "Be in church whenever the doors are open").
* "Don't cut out anything. Take on more instead."
* "Make yourself available and God will use you."
* "Work on becoming godly."

All voices in unison: "There's always more you can do to become the woman God wants you to be."

Our response: "I give up. I'm tired of working toward godliness. The harder I work, the less I produce. It's a no-win situation."

A Lone Voice: "That's because you're listening to what everybody else is saying. My emphasis is on who you are, not on what you are doing. When you have a personal relationship with God through His Son, Jesus Christ, you can be at rest and still be 'productive.'"

Accentuating the Positive

While on a speaking engagement in the South, I was privileged to stay with Merci, a lovely woman greatly respected in her church. After the seminar, she invited her friend Lisa to join us for coffee. As we took our seats at Merci's table, we couldn't help noticing the pears in her centerpiece. How large they were! And how delicious they proved to be! As we ate, I knew a spiritual application was in the making.

"Christians are known by their fruit," Lisa began. "But I'd like to know what the Bible means by that. Is fruit what we are becoming or what we are doing?"

There was a pause.

"I'm not sure I can quote the passage properly," Merci ventured, "but I'll try. 'The fruit of the spirit is love, joy, peace, patience, kindness, goodness, faithfulness, gentleness, and self-control' [Gal. 5:22–23]. In other words, it's what we are."

"But in another place—I can't remember where—the Bible associates fruit with 'every good work,'" Lisa interjected.

"Which comes first though," I probed, "what we are or what we do? A pear tree is a pear tree before it produces pears, isn't it? Being precedes doing, right?"

"Right!" Merci confirmed. "But for a tree to produce at all, it needs a good root system. Once that is established and blossoms begin to appear, it needs pruning. You don't get pears of that caliber," she nodded toward the centerpiece, "without some pretty drastic cutting back."

"Selective elimination—is that what you're talking about?" I asked, already knowing the answer.

"Of course," Merci replied. "When I agreed to be circle leader this year, I knew I'd have to give up teaching my Sunday School class."

"But doesn't it hurt to cut out something productive?" Lisa moaned.

"You bet. But look what you get," Merci motioned toward the large fruit, "better quality."

As I pondered the many but small "pears" in my own life, I knew I needed to prune. But I winced at the idea of pain.

I guess Lisa did, too, for she said, "God chooses some rather reluctant trees to produce the fruit of His likeness, doesn't He?"

"The weakest," Merci answered.

"Why the weakest?" Lisa asked. "Why doesn't He choose the strongest?"

"He could, but there's a danger," Merci answered. "Strong personalities steal His glory. They get the credit He deserves."

"Wait a minute," Lisa interrupted. "I want to make sure I've got this: God can use the strong but prefers the weak. Is that what you're saying?"

"Not me," Merci emphasized. "The Bible. But there's a condition: the weak have to yield their weaknesses."

"That's hard to do," I commiserated, "because there's a risk. I mean, who wants to fail?"

"That's where the local church comes in," Lisa contributed. "It's there to equip us. It provides instruction, support, fellowship, and worship. That's why whenever something's going on, I'm in my pew. I don't want to miss out on a single blessing."

"I hear you," Merci responded. "And I too am grateful for the fellowship of believers. But the pressure to go, go, go and do, do, do gets to me. At times it overshadows God's desire for me to 'become.' When the Bible commands, 'Be holy,' I don't think it means 'Go to holy places and do holy things.' I think it means 'Manifest the likeness of the Lord Jesus Christ.' If you can do that while you're 'going' and 'doing,' great. But if not, it's time to cut back."

"Do I detect a mixture of truth and error in the pressure the church is placing upon us?" I asked. "Could we spend some time sorting out which is which? The essence of Christianity seems to be at stake here."

"I'm not going anywhere," Merci laughed.

"I'd love it!" Lisa enthused.

So the three of us continued our discussion.

Overstatement and Truth

* *The FCW thinks*, "What I do is measurable. What I am is not. So I will go with what counts."

The Lone Voice whispers, "To God what you are becoming is infinitely more valuable than what you are accomplishing. You are chosen to be "conformed to the image of His Son" (Rom. 8:29).

* *The FCW thinks*, "Every time something is going on at church, I have to be involved. I don't want people to think I'm backsliding."

The Lone Voice whispers, "You're listening to others again— voices that equate spirituality with sitting in a pew. Listen to the One who looks past church involvement into the heart.

"Church membership carries a weighty responsibility and should not be taken lightly. Involvement is a must. However, there is such a thing as involvement for involvement's sake, which can become a dangerous substitute for Christian growth. So choose to do some things without feeling you have to do everything."

* *The FCW thinks*, "I've got to keep up with all my activities. To cut back on anything 'Christian' would be displeasing to God."

The Lone Voice whispers, "It's displeasing to God when you refuse to cut back. He's the One who says, 'Whatever you do, work at it with all your heart' (Col. 3:23). When you eliminate in order to concentrate ('prune'), you become focused instead of fragmented. Your fruit is large and tastes sweet to everyone, especially to the Lord."

* *The FCW thinks*, "If I present myself to God, He will use me, warts and all."

The Lone Voice whispers, "True. As the saying goes, He'll use 'any old bush that burns.' But He prefers to use the usable. The sensitive, self-controlled woman will be more effective than the one who is self-promoting, arrogant or abrasive—regardless of how willing she is to serve. God doesn't put Christians to use hoping to develop in them His characteristics—although, admittedly, this sometimes does happen. Rather, may the Christlike qualities come first, then be evident in what Christians do."

* *The FCW thinks*, "I'm afraid to launch out into unchartered waters, especially when the stakes are eternal. What if I fail?"

The Lone Voice whispers, "Isn't the kingdom of God worth a risk? What will happen if you don't try? You'll just get older, and your potential will shrivel. You will have missed the opportunity to grow.

"Rare is the person who comes into the Christian life qualified to serve the risen Lord. Most people get stretched into doing it. Actually, stretching can be fun. For when you're in the Father's hands, 'attaining to the whole measure of the fullness of Christ' (Eph. 4:13) becomes a fail-safe adventure—something exciting."

* *The FCW thinks*, "I want to be a woman known for her spirituality. If I take one spiritual fruit at a time and work at it, eventually I'll possess all the characteristics of a godly woman."

The Lone Voice whispers, "Impossible. Fruit can't be worked up. You never hear a tree say, 'I've got to produce a pear today.' Rather, it yields its branches to the power within and manifests its nature automatically.

"For you, this may mean admitting, 'I'm about to blow it, Lord. But I don't want to. Here, take my mouth, my hands, and my heart. Do through me what I cannot do without You.' Then watch the miracle happen."

A Divine Perspective

As I was contemplating the tension between what a Christian is supposed to be and what a Christian is expected to do, I decided to leaf through my Bible to see where God places His emphasis. I stopped at Psalm 1: "[The righteous man] is like a tree planted by streams of water, which yields its fruit in season and whose leaf does not wither. Whatever he does prospers" (v. 3).

God begins with what we are, I noticed, and proceeds to what we do, guaranteeing what we do will be a blessing as long as we stay close to water. Since water seems to be the key to a tree's prosperity, I checked the previous verse to make sure I understood what water symbolizes. Sure enough, "water" is "the law of the Lord," upon which those who are blessed meditate (see v. 2).

The prophet Isaiah verifies this symbolism when he says, "As the rain . . . [comes] down from heaven and [does] not return to it without watering the earth and making it bud and flourish, so that it yields seed for the sower and bread for the eater, so is my word that goes out from my mouth" (55:10–11). Holy Scripture, then, is the key to my flourishing, I affirmed, but it is my job to keep absorbing it.

As I paused to take this in, I couldn't help thinking of another Scripture that deals with trees and water: Ezekiel 47; so I turned there to see if any new insight might leap out at me. I decided to put myself in Ezekiel's shoes and let the guide who was leading him into deeper truth lead me. He did.

First, he pointed out a river. I watched as it flowed past my feet in its rush toward the sea. Then he pointed to trees lining the river's banks. I counted a "great number" of them (see v. 7). "These are fruit-bearing trees," the guide explained. "Their leaves will not wither nor will their fruit fail. Every month they will bear."

"Every month?" I queried as I remembered being overwhelmed by trees that produced once a year. "These trees produce every month?"

"Yes," the guide answered. "They show what they are all the time. There's not a minute when you're left wondering. The secret to their abundant productivity, though, is in their location near the water." I nodded.

"This water, you will notice, flows from the 'sanctuary' (see v. 12)—from the spot where the Lord is enthroned, from the place where the believer meets Him in personal worship. The tree's connection to the sanctuary is what gives it its supernatural power.

Do you understand?"

I did. But I knew there was more for me, and I wanted all of it, so I didn't say a word. I just continued to listen to the guide. He was concluding his discourse on the trees. "Their fruit will serve for food and their leaves for healing," he said.

As I processed the information in that concluding statement, I had no trouble applying the part about food. I had repeatedly asked God to make the fruit of my relationship with Him a source of spiritual sustenance to others. But "leaves for healing?" I questioned. Then I deduced, "These trees must be designed for a lot more than just fruit-bearing."

"They are," my guide affirmed. "Although fruit is foremost because it manifests the nature of the trees, leaves have a vital function also. In them is the power to relieve pain and promote healing."

As I thought about this, I found myself wanting to be a "total tree," showing the world not only my new nature but my renewed concern for those who are hurting. "Thank You, Guide," I whispered.

Then I said to myself, "What kind of tree would I want to be if given a choice?"

Certainly not one that's prickly or sharp, I decided. Nor one that people stare at because of its odd shape. Nor one known for retaining water (I don't like that bloated feeling). I also wouldn't choose to be a tree that strangles its host; after all, as a public speaker, I sometimes stay in private homes.

No, I would choose to be a eucalyptus, one of those tall, stately trees, splashed with color, silky smooth to touch. A tree that sports fragrant, aromatic leaves. A tree that cuddles koalas, heals the sick, and provides a stimulant for folks who need a little "pick-me-up."

But mine is not the choice to make, I know. Such choices belong to a sovereign Lord. He has a use for every tree, regardless of its size, shape, or manner in which it presents itself. This truth became even clearer as I researched "trees" in my trusty encyclopedia.

Trees are one of the few living things that never stop growing, I learned—I love this truth! And as they mature, they serve some wonderful functions:

    1. Trees evoke wonder. People often stop just to look at them. Perhaps in the process they contemplate the

Creator. Who knows?

2. Trees provide shade. People who feel they are being stifled can pause under a tree's canopy and catch their breath.

3. Trees produce food. The hungry are attracted to their fruit. And should a passerby reach out and partake, his void will be filled.

4. Trees make life easier. They provide oil, gum, resin, syrup, drink, spices, perfumes, dyes, paper, cloth, and a host of other delights.

In short, trees are a blessing to pilgrims on Planet Earth.

But there are more treasures in the study of trees. Every tree has four distinct parts, I discovered, each as important as the next. First, roots provide an anchor, so when winds sweep through and rains beat down, an extensive root system renders the tree unshakable. While the tree will certainly feel the effects of the storm and may even suffer damage, it won't shift its position. It will stay put.

Roots also provide the tree's contact point with water. They collect this source of life, send it up to the leaves and, in return, receive energy to keep the process going. I found myself marveling at how intricate a transportation system a tree has.

Actually, the second part, the wood, is what acts as the conduit through which the tree's sap and food pass, I learned. But the wood does much more than transport nourishment. It provides material for building, fuel for warmth, and support for the weary.

"I love being called a tree," I exclaimed as I delved further into my study.

Third, the tree's bark is analogous to our skin. It serves as a protection from injury and disease. It also provides a substance which has both commercial and medicinal uses: tannin.

Last comes the canopy of leaves that take energy from the sunlight and make food. In this canopy, or crown, cones, flowers, and fruit are produced. They all bear seeds, any one of which has the power to produce another tree. What potential! I marveled. It sent chills up and down my spine.

"Lord," I found myself praying, "it's an honor to have You call me a tree. I must say, though, I identify more with a grasshopper [see chap. 1], but it's time to make a switch, I guess. Grasshoppers *do*; trees *are*, yet in their inactivity trees are used. In fact, they are used more than grasshoppers will ever be!

"Make me a sturdy tree," I continued. "I want to send my roots down deep. I want to experience the power of living water flowing through me. I want to produce leaves that are useful and fruit that is large and succulent. Whatever it takes, Lord, please do it, even if it hurts. I want to be a tribute to the One who has planted me near the source of life and provides everything I need to grow into the full measure of my intended stature."

What Can We Do to Change Things?

Make a list of "godly" people. As we make our selections, let's remember to concentrate on what these people are like, rather than what they have accomplished. Is it hard to come up with names? We might ask, would our names appear on anybody's "godly list"? Let's think of list makers at work, at church, and at home—uh-oh!

What characteristics do these "godly" people have? The most important, probably, is a healthy self-abasement. They are not out to impress others with their holiness. Yet they do—quite naturally—as they focus on yielding to their Lord. They seem to have learned the secret of being "actively passive" (to borrow a phrase from Francis Schaeffer). They neither try to do God's work for Him ("I've got to show Christian love today"), nor do they sit back and expect God to do His work without them ("Father, turning me into a loving person will require a miracle!"). No, they just open themselves to the power within and let it have full rein. We, then, as observers, are privileged to see, even to taste, their fruit.

Check for personal Christlike qualities. We'll never get to the root of our problem if we're not honest with ourselves. This requires asking two tough questions. First, am I guilty of doing to escape becoming? Second, do I substitute church work for personal holiness?

Manifesting the character of Jesus Christ, which, we remember, is God's goal for every believer, comes through relationship, not through effort. Just as healthy trees produce fruit because their branches, trunk, and roots are all connected, so a Christian woman produces the Savior's likeness as she becomes open to His power.

Do a top-to-toe check on how we come across to others:

- Thoughts: Do I evidence the "mind of Christ," or do I give the impression of being a self-centered scheme machine?
- Sight: Does it appear I am viewing the world from Christ's perspective or through my own limited peephole?
- Hearing: Do I heed cries of pain, or am I deaf to people's groanings?
- Words: Do I "speak the truth in love," or do I cut people down in anger?
- Actions: Do I reach out to comfort, or do I hold people at arm's length?
- Heart: Does forgiveness flow through me, or am I bitter and resentful?
- Walk: Do I follow in the footsteps of my Lord, or do I strike out in my own direction?

Bottom line: When people look at me, do they see Jesus Christ? Do I want them to?

Be our own fruit inspectors. Ask, "Does my life today evidence more fruit of the Spirit (Gal. 5:22–23) than it did when I first trusted Christ?

- more love (toward difficult people)?
- more joy (even in sorrow)?
- more peace (in the midst of chaos)?
- more patience (while I'm waiting)?
- more kindness (when I feel like lashing out)?
- more goodness (where sin abounds)?
- more faithfulness (when everybody else is giving up)?
- more gentleness (when others are abrasive toward me)?
- more self-control (when emotions threaten to take over)?"

As we do our check, let's be encouraged by how far we have come rather than discouraged by how far we have to go. The Bible says, "Though outwardly we are wasting away, yet inwardly we are being renewed day by day" (see 2 Cor. 4:16). What an encouragement to keep pressing on!

Yield our weaknesses to God. Weak areas are part of the human design, intentionally built in by the Creator to make sure the creature doesn't steal His glory. Never does this truth impact us more powerfully than when we face a situation we cannot handle. At those times we have two choices: we can either give up or we can give over. Giving up indicates defeat, perhaps permanently, while giving over signals victory. The sovereign Lord has taken control, and His power has now become mine. In fact, His power is "made perfect" in weakness, the Bible says (see 2 Cor. 12:9). No wonder the apostle Paul boasts, "I delight in weakness. . . . For when I am weak, then I am strong" (v. 10). Yes, he is. And so are we.

Prune for bigger fruit. This involves removing not only those branches that are non-productive but some that are productive as well. When we prune, we are left with fewer places on which to concentrate our efforts and, consequently, fewer pears. But the pears that are produced have more meat. They show observers what a pear tree should be—and what a pear tree can be when the Caretaker is allowed to take over.

Confirmation from God's Word

1. Read John 15:1–17, NASB describing the Vine and the branches.
2. Ponder:
   - The message of verse 2 is "Bear fruit!" while the message of verse 4 is "You cannot bear fruit." Why this apparent contradiction?
   - If a branch tries to produce fruit by itself—without a continuing relationship with the Vine—what will be the result (v. 4)?
   - Notice the progression from no fruit, to fruit, to more fruit, to much fruit. What happens to a branch that produces no fruit (v. 2)? To one that produces some fruit (v. 2)? How does a branch go from bearing fruit to bearing much fruit (v. 5)? Does "abiding" require work or yieldedness?
   - What keeps the connection between the Vine and the branches clean (v. 3)? What's the benefit of a clean connection (v. 7)?
3. What positive effects should the FCW enjoy from learning to "abide in" (have continuing fellowship with) Jesus Christ?

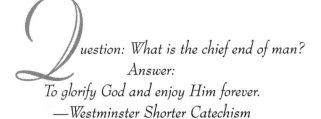

Question: What is the chief end of man?
Answer:
To glorify God and enjoy Him forever.
—Westminster Shorter Catechism

12

Set Me Free to Glorify God

"Then you shall know the truth, and the truth will set you free."
John 8:32

The mood was somber that day as Lee and I and our three young boys ambled through the cemetery behind an old church. The grass was high and the tombstones weathered. But many inscriptions were still visible.

"What kinds of lives did these people live?" I wondered as I stepped reverently from grave to grave. "How did they die? Does anyone remember them?

"Not long ago they were as alive as I am: men, women, and children—with families, careers, and hobbies. They got up in the morning, breathed deeply, and went about their various activities. Now they are gone, never to anticipate, hope, share, fear, or conduct business again. How fragile life is. How short!"

"Look at this gravestone, Mom!" Greg shouted, piercing my reverie. "It says, 'Here lies my be-lov-ed wife! What's be-lov-ed mean, Mom?"

"It means to be loved, silly," Jeff teased as he examined the stones at his own feet.

Then exhilarated by a discovery, he shouted, "Here's another one! This lady was 'a dedicated mother.' Are you a dedicated mother, Mom?"

"Of course she is!" Dirk exclaimed. "She takes care of us, doesn't she?"

Then a slab caught Dirk's eye. He paused, then concluded, "This woman must have lived in a church. It says, 'Found in death where found in life: in her family pew.'"

"Why would somebody want to live in a church, Mom?" Dirk asked.

"She didn't live there," Lee answered from a few feet away. "She probably just spent a lot of time there."

Then Lee pointed out an epitaph of a different sort. "Respected community leader," it read.

"Nice tribute," he declared.

As I continued my stroll up and down the rows of tombstones, I decided to concentrate on epitaphs describing women. There were more tributes to wives, mothers, church members, and community leaders—all significant statements.

"But where is a tribute to a woman's Christianity, regardless of how she manifested it?" I wondered. "Why is there no epitaph that reads, "A life lived out for God's glory, period!"?

My ponderings deepened as I turned the corner of the church. "I wonder what Jesus' tombstone would have said," I mused, "if He had remained in the grave long enough to have one, that is?"

I knew I couldn't compare the life of the sinless One to the lives of these ordinary human beings beneath my feet, but I thought about what Jesus said to the Father right before He went to the cross, and it brought me up short. "I have brought You glory by completing the work You gave me to do," He stated.

"What an example!" I thought. "In one short statement we have a clearly defined purpose, a declaration that every task was focused on achieving it, and a sense that in the end life was not lived in vain. A life's work had been completed.

"How I would love to have such a banner over my own life," I said wistfully. "Think of it: 'I have brought You glory, my heavenly Father. I have finished the tasks You assigned me on earth.'"

"Will I ever be able to say that?" I wondered. "Ever? The messages I'm receiving are confusing me."

Listen to the Many Voices

* "Strive to be all you can. God is glorified in the pursuit of excellence."

* "Work to earn heavenly crowns. This is pleasing to God."

* "Christianity needs people who make things happen for God. There are too many people sitting on the sidelines."

* "Search diligently for God's will. If you miss it you'll miss life's purpose."

All voices in unison: "Do all you can for the cause of Christ and trust God to be glorified through your efforts."

Our response: "Something's wrong here. The end is justifying the means. How can God be glorified when He is left out of the process?"

A Lone Voice: "He can't. But very few Christians realize this. The fact that you do shows you are making progress. Just a few more steps and you'll be out freedom's door."

Accentuating the Positive

El looked tan and relaxed in her golf shorts and hat as she stood there holding some sprigs of mint.

"For your iced tea," she explained, knowing we drink it almost every night.

"Thanks," I said, inviting her in. "Got a minute?"

"Sure," she agreed as she pulled a chair from the kitchen table.

"I'm hung up on the last chapter of my book," I began. "Since you used to be a medical technician and are now in the financial world, I think you're the right person to ask a question or two."

"Shoot!" El exclaimed as she placed her elbows on the table and leaned forward.

"I'm wondering how the 'pursuit of excellence' craze that is currently driving the corporate world relates to Christianity. Is excellence an acceptable motivation for God's people, or is it too 'worldly'?"

"It depends on what's behind it," El answered, "God's glory or man's. It's possible for a Christian to do things in the name of Christ and yet do them for self-advancement."

"Sad but true," I agreed.

"Yet," El persisted, "the Originator of the standard of excellence is none other than the Lord Himself. So since He set it, He must expect His followers to pursue it. Therefore, we must seize every opportunity to let our lights shine, don't you think? In a world of mediocrity, we can be different, we can stand out, we can excel, and hopefully, we can draw attention to the One who is motivating us.

"Let me give you a personal example," she continued. "In the hospital where I worked, some technicians did just enough to get by. I couldn't. I was a Christian. Mistakes can happen—and do. And I am not a perfectionist. But I always tried to do my best, even when the job was routine. I would have been devastated if something important slipped by me and it cost a life."

"Does this dedication to excellence apply now to your work in the financial world?"

"Money is not as important as human life," El emphasized. "So the same type of pressure isn't there. But I do take my business seriously. After all, whatever I'm doing, analyzing blood or investing in the stock market, I'm ultimately serving the Lord, right?"

"That's what the Bible says," I smiled. "But tell me, what motivates you?"

"Gratitude," El replied. "I'm so grateful Christ died for me that I want to honor Him."

"So for you, God is the beginning, the middle, and the end of everything," I summarized.

"That's a good way to put it," El agreed.

"Are you working for crowns at judgment?" I ventured.

El hesitated. "Not really. As I said before, I'm more motivated by gratitude. But I know people who are motivated by rewards."

"Do you consider this a healthy motivation?" I probed.

"As long as it's not the main one. I would hate to think I'm doing something because of what I'm going to get out of it."

"I would like to talk further about how such pressure fractures us. Can you spare an hour or so?"

"I sure can," El smiled.

Overstatement and Truth

* *The FCW thinks*, "Excellence should be my goal. I'll make God proud by being the best."

The Lone Voice whispers, "In God's eyes how you achieve a goal is as important as the goal itself. If you sin in the pursuit of excellence, God cannot be honored. But if you conduct yourself excellently, whether or not you achieve what you set out to do, God will be glorified."

* *The FCW thinks*, "I must work hard in order to hear 'well done' on Judgment Day."

The Lone Voice whispers, "Let God worry about Judgment Day. You worry about the here and now. Are you living for Christ today? That's the question."

* *The FCW thinks*, "Those who are really glorifying God work to bring His kingdom to reality. They don't wait for things to happen. They cause them."

The Lone Voice whispers, "While Christian activists can further God's plan, their activity may not always be God-glorifying. You need a close relationship to the Savior in order to reflect His desires in what you do."

* *The FCW thinks*, "The sooner I discover God's will for my life the better. I don't want to live in vain."

The Lone Voice whispers, "God's will is not a mysterious something for which you must search. When you discover life's purpose, you discover the will of God. After that comes the challenge of living it. Obedience is never easy. It's easier to keep searching."

* *The FCW thinks*, "I'll make my plans and execute them. Then I'll pray for God's stamp of approval."

The Lone Voice whispers, "Danger! You're making God an asterisk to life when, in fact, He is the whole statement. He doesn't want you to act, then hope for His approval. He wants you to seek His approval first, then act with His blessing."

A Divine Perspective

"Uh-oh!" I moaned as I ran the comb through my hair and a strange strand appeared. "Time to start coloring it, I guess."

As I stood staring into the mirror on my thirty-third birthday, I knew it would be a memorable occasion. It was. It was the first time I came face to face with the dreaded effects of aging—in myself, that is—and I would not forget it. Plus, I realized I was now at the age Jesus was when He died. Thirty-three years was all the time He had to do His work on earth. Yet He met the deadline. He finished His work.

I looked around me. "My work is never finished," I lamented. "In the time allotted to Jesus He changed the course of history. I am still changing beds! And thirty-three years of my life have gone by."

When I expressed my frustration to my mother, she corrected me. "Jesus didn't do His work in thirty-three years," she said. "He did it in three. The first thirty were preparation. His impact was the result of a short but concentrated effort."

"Thanks, Mom!" I felt like saying. "Now I feel even worse." But I was silent as I contemplated funnelling my first thirty-three years into my future, concentrating on whatever God might want me to do in my allotted time.

Since that day I have looked into the mirror on many occasions—with increasing frustration. I mean, when you press on your eyelid and it stays depressed, that can be very depressing. Or when you notice your neck looks like plucked chicken skin, it can take the pluck right out of you.

But we are not without help. Cosmetics to the rescue! Lots of them. First, we line up the moisturizers. When you're trying to turn a prune back into the plum it used to be, you need all the moisturizers you can get. Next come the fillers, the cover-ups, the shadows, and the blushes. We apply them with utmost care.

Then it's the body's turn. "She ain't what she used to be," we sigh as we assess creases, sags, and bulges. But not to despair! There's a new fitness center in town that's been hawking reconstruction miracles. "We'll help you sink in where you now stick out," they're promising, "and stick out where you now sink in" (or something like that).

Do we want to make the switch? Maybe a good workout or two will do the trick.

Nah. Let's just go with what we've got. Less pain.

"Where's that new pair of pantyhose?" we wonder out loud. "You know, the one with the extra strong control top?"

If the pantyhose don't work, we can always reach for our elastic unmentionable and coax, squeeze, and shove our bulges into it. It's those ham shanks that are giving us trouble. Ever since they started degenerating into spongy waffles, they've become quite a challenge. But this latex expands, we're assured, and restrains its contents—for up to eighteen hours!

Uh-oh! What is pushed in at one spot is destined to pop out another. That's the first law of body dynamics, isn't it? So let's chose our upper-body-hold-it-all-in-garments carefully, going for one that not only supports but "lifts and separates."

Ah yes, we're contained at last, like overstuffed sausages that don't dare bend.

Now we're ready for the trimmings. We reach for something comfortable. (Something has to be comfortable, doesn't it?). We make sure it matches our skin tones. (We've been color analyzed, you know.) Now let's accentuate the garment with a flashy scarf, a classy belt, and matching heels. Then we look again into the mirror. Amazing! Miracles still happen on Planet Earth.

It's a losing battle though. And it's all Eve's fault! If she hadn't plucked that fruit from the forbidden tree, we might still be firm, succulent plums—just as she was when she was first created. Talk about momentous days! Think about that day in the Garden of Eden when God breathed into man the breath of life.

Then Eve was created from Adam's rib—a beautifully symbolic gesture on God's part. She was meant to walk by her husband's side, be protected by his arm, and be held close to his heart.

Since she also spent time with her Creator, was sheltered by His love, and encouraged to reflect His glory, she must have exuded godly purpose in everything she did. It must have showed in her walk, sparkled from her eyes, and glowed from her face. No moisturizers needed. She was manifesting eternal life—life from the inside out.

One day, however, all that changed. Eve's motivation turned to self-glory. Wanting to be in control, she reached for fruit from the tree of the knowledge of good and evil and ate it, assimilating its power. "Now I can determine what's good," she boasted. Little did she know how her decision would come back to haunt her.

The change began on the inside. Instead of contentment, joy, and hope, she started experiencing tension, anxiety, and despair. As we all know, you can't harbor negative feelings very long before they start working their way to the surface. So it was with Eve.

One day as she was combing her beautiful hair, a strand came out that was different from the rest. And we think *we* were shocked at the sight of our first gray hair! Imagine what it would be like if you had never seen one before—on anybody!

Unfortunately, Eve passed her problem on, not only her rebellion against God's purposes but the effects of that rebellion. We see those effects every morning in the bathroom mirror. They are confirmed in the mirror of God's Word. "All men are like grass," the Bible says (I presume this means all women too), "and their glory is like the flowers of the field; the grass withers and the flowers fall, but the word of the Lord stands forever" (1 Pet. 1:24–25).

"I'm comforted by the fact You recognize our plight," I said to the Lord when I discovered this verse.

"Turn to the Book of Ecclesiastes," His Spirit seemed to answer, "and I will show you more."

So I did, anticipating God's commentary on the meaninglessness of life without Him. As I read through His statement on the effects of aging (see 12:3–5), I couldn't help adding my own running commentary. The two commentaries progressed something like this:

God was speaking first. "You know you are getting older," He was saying, "when the keepers of the house tremble." Realizing the Lord was speaking metaphorically, I held out the arms of my "house" to see how steady they were.

"Not bad," I announced. "Let's go to the next effect of aging."

" . . . and the strong men stoop," the Lord continued. Since I've been struggling with degenerative osteoarthritis for several years, I had no trouble identifying with this description. "Score one!" I conceded. "Let's keep going down Your list, Father." We did.

" . . . when the grinders cease because they are few," He said next. Well, I did lose my wisdom teeth a few years ago—and the smarts that go with them. But since I live in an age of preventive dentistry, my tooth loss is not as bad as it could be. "Thank You, Lord," I breathed. "Next?"

" . . . and those looking through the windows grow dim." (I don't have cataracts yet, I found myself thinking, and I'm grateful for that. But this floater in my left eye is driving me nuts, especially as I'm writing these very words. "What's next on Your inventory, Lord?"

" . . . when the doors to the streets are closed and the sound of the grinding fades." It must be awful, I decided, when you can't even hear yourself chew. I haven't degenerated that far, but I do have trouble catching a discussion around a table in a crowded restaurant. "Next item, Lord?"

" . . . when men rise up at the sound of birds but all their songs grow faint." Insomnia must be the pits, I commiserated, especially when you can't enjoy the sounds of the morning you're awaking to. It's true I don't sleep as well as I used to (hot flashes, you know), but I really can't complain. There are others who hardly sleep at all. "How many more items on Your list, Lord?"

" . . . when men are afraid of heights and of danger in the streets." Well, since we live on the fourteenth floor of a high rise, I can't claim to have a problem with heights. But "danger in the streets"—who isn't afraid of that, especially those of us who live in the greater New York City area? "Let's proceed, Father."

" . . . when the almond tree blossoms." Yes, the white top has come to me also, but thank You, Lord, for the wherewithal to change its color. "Next item in this degenerative process?"

" . . . and the grasshopper drags himself along." (The grasshopper won't give up, will he? At least he's not hopping quite so much these days. Maybe he's content to be still and look up, past the blades of grass, into the eyes of his Creator.) "Next?"

" . . . then man goes to his eternal home and mourners go about the streets."

"Father God, this is a poignant list—with a very sobering end," I exclaimed as I finished reading and mentally commenting on what I had read. "As a mature woman, I appreciate these descriptions of the frustrating aging process. But the women for whom I am writing this book are, for the most part, young. They haven't yet experienced depressed eyelids, chicken-skin necks, and waffle thighs."

"They will," the answer came. "Actually, if you examine the passage carefully, you will see that I wrote it for the young, for they can heed My concluding statement: 'Remember your Creator in the days of your youth, *before* the days of trouble come . . . *before* the sun and the light of the moon and the stars grow dark . . . *before* the silver cord is severed or the golden bowl is broken, *before* the pitcher is shattered at the spring, or the wheel broken at the well . . .' (12:1–2,6,emphasis added). They are the ones who can still make changes."

What Can We Do to Change Things?

Write our own obituaries. Let's start with how we would like them to read. Then let's write them the way they will probably read when composed by (1) our husband, (2) our kids, (3) our pastor, (4) our friends, (5) our neighbors, and last (6) our Creator. Where are the biggest discrepancies?

As we write, let's remember life's essence lies not in what we have done but rather in who we are. Jesus Christ, we remember, did not go everywhere He was asked to go. Nor did He do everything He was asked to do. But He went where the Father wanted Him to go and did what the Father wanted Him to do. He knew the truth of the maxim, "You have all the time you need to do the will of God." The will of God, of course, is to bring the Father glory, sometimes by just being. In that being lies the significance of who Jesus Christ is.

Likewise, it is from who we are that our life's work flows. This work may be glamorous or routine, visible or behind the scenes, far-reaching or close by, conceptual or detailed, active or passive, sacred or secular. The category is not important. What is important is whether it's God's work, done exclusively for God's glory.

Sometimes I ask, "What is Your work for me, Lord, right now, today, this moment?"

I am always surprised when He answers, "What you are doing." God sanctifies ordinary tasks performed by the most ordinary people, doesn't He?

Reaffirm life's purpose. "I'm here to glorify You, Lord, and to enjoy my relationship with You forever." God "created" us, "formed" us, and "made" us, He says, for His own glory (see Isa. 43:7). But there's a corollary to this powerful concept: the joy of intimate fellowship with the Creator. It is something that can be experienced all the time, regardless of one's lot in life. While a job or a circumstance may be distasteful, we can still enjoy God in it. And the peace that comes from this bonding carries us through.

God promises to be present in our every mood. When we are tense, He relaxes us. When we are sad, He lifts our spirits. When we are exhausted or sick, He scoops us into His arms and whispers "I love you." We don't have to do anything but let Him minister. What blessings there are in a personal relationship with God!

When tempted to act independently, stop. Let's first ask:

- Am I acting as if God exists to glorify me?
- Am I trying to use God to promote my own purposes?
- Am I out for number one?

- Am I cloaking my personal ambitions with church work?
- Whose will is being served anyway?

How twisted our thinking sometimes becomes! How subtle we are as we mock God's grace! In this day of easy-believism we "receive" Jesus Christ for what He can do for us, then we "claim" whatever He has for us—things that will make our lives easier, of course.

Is it not a privilege to serve the King of kings, even if there are no visible benefits at all? But the amazing thing is that there are benefits in abundance. This is grace. And it is ours. So let's express our gratitude to God by living our faith.

Take an attitude inventory, especially when serving at church. Let's ask:

- Do I resent having to do this?
- Am I bitter toward those who asked me?
- Am I justifying my feelings by rationalizing that I'm doing this for God?

If we answer yes to any of these questions, it's time to re-examine our motivation and reestablish on-going communication with our Creator. He is always there, ready to forgive, and anxious to grant us a new beginning.

Pray for motivation that is pure. Let's remember it's acceptable, even advisable, to be honest with God about how we feel. It's okay to dump our frustrations on Him. For example:

"I'm having trouble sorting things out, Lord. If I get involved doing something that honors You (but not in an obvious way), I tend to think it's not important. This is wrong, isn't it?

"When I take time for myself, I feel guilty. I know I shouldn't, but I still do.

"Sometimes I get so starry-eyed about serving a good cause, I jump right in. Then I find out it's not for me. But I don't know how to get out. What glory is there for You in situations like this?

"Other times my pride gets wounded. I get in over my head, then feel so awful I can't live with myself. Why can't I control things better?

"When I do something stupid and pay for it, I feel as if You are punishing me for stepping out of Your will. This is bondage, I know, but I can't help it.

"I'm getting older, Lord, and I really don't want to find I've lived my whole life in vain. So search me and know my heart; try and know my thoughts" (see Ps.139:23). Refine, cleanse, and purify my motives with Your consuming fire."

Then step back, and watch the changes occur.

Be obedient to God's revealed will. We don't know everything. In fact, there are times when we think we don't know anything. But let's take heart. The Bible says, "For now we see through a glass darkly" (1 Cor. 13:12, KJV). How true! And our vision problem is not due entirely to failing eyesight or cataracts. There are things we simply cannot envision because God is keeping the future clouded—deliberately.

Why do people seek to know the future anyway? What a burden! Think how Jesus, who knew the hour of His death, must have felt as that hour drew near. We are told His stress was so great He sweat "drops of blood" (see Luke 22:44). And He was the Son of God. He was able to handle it!

By a stroke of divine grace, we do not know the hour of our death—or any other hour for that matter. Some things are part of God's will concealed, but we do know where we are now and what we are about. So in a sense, God has "made known to us the mystery of His will" (Eph. 1:9). He tells us plainly we are to live "for the praise of his glory" (v. 12). Do we need to know more? Isn't this, in itself, a full-time job?

Concentrate on living for today and leaving tomorrow to God. There is an urgency as far as the kingdom of God is concerned, and every Christian is aware of it. The age of God's grace is drawing to a close rapidly. We do not know how much time we have. So we want to make the most of every moment.

Urgency, however, can work against us. It can drive us to overinvest in "Christian projects." Then one day when it's too late, we realize we've been pushing just to "finish the job." God's glory has become an addendum to our efforts, and enjoyment of our personal relationship with Him almost nonexistent.

Life is to be lived—and lived fully, moment by precious moment. If God grants us many years, fine. If not, that's fine too, for He has laid the road of our lives and walks each step beside us, even those steps that lead us through the valley of death. Then He presents us faultless before the throne of His Father's glory. Hallelujah, what a Savior, what a Lord!

Confirmation from God's Word

1. Read 2 Corinthians 3:17–4:18, NASB describing treasure in earthen vessels.

Note: 2 Corinthians 3–4 contains the greatest concentration of the words "glorify" and "glorious" in the Bible.

Highlight these words: (While in the wilderness, Moses asked God to show him His glory, and God answered, "I will cause all my goodness to pass in front of you" [Ex. 33:19]. The glory of God and the character of God [His "goodness"], then, become synonymous.)

2. Two functions of the Holy Spirit are mentioned in 3:17–18. What are they?

- What are some of the freedoms you have experienced since becoming a Christian?
- Think of a recent situation in which you responded with a Christlikeness you didn't know was in you. To what do you attribute this response?

3. What is a prerequisite for reflecting God's glory (3:18)? What hope does this verse hold for women who are serious about their faith?

4. According to verse 6, what two parts of the body are capable of "shining" with God's glory? Should Christians be able to recognize those of "like precious faith"—in supermarkets, banks, airports, sports arenas, wherever? Why or why not?

5. Name some hindrances to Christian growth, things that could cause us to "lose heart" (see vv. 4:1, 16). How can we combat these hindrances (Note the reason for the "therefores")?

6. To have a successful ministry, what three things must we do (see v. 2)? Why is each of these necessary?

7. Who is out to cause discouragement, confusion, and spiritual blindness (v. 4)?

8. Where is the power to defeat the enemy (v. 7)? How do we appropriate this power?

9. To combat the pressures that cause fracturing (4:8–9), where must our focus be (4:18)?

10. What should this passage do for the FCW?

Epilogue

Eight-year-old Jessica is working on her favorite puzzle again. As she slips the last piece into place, she stands back to admire her work.

"Mommy," she shouts toward the kitchen, "come see Snow White. She's all put together."

Laurie enters the room, towel in hand. Her eyes fall upon the completed puzzle, every piece aligned.

"That's perfect, Jessica," she encourages. "I'm very proud of you."

Laurie thinks no more of the incident until that night when she goes to bed. While she is asleep, she dreams. She finds herself visualizing the familiar game table in her den with the pieces of her photograph scattered upon it. Is her previous nightmare going to start up where it left off? She shudders to think of it.

Standing around the table in this dream are the same folks who cut up her treasured picture: her husband, her children, her pastor, and others. Only this time, they are trying to reassemble the fragments. She sighs with relief.

Her loved ones seem to know where the pieces should go, but they can't figure out how to make them stay put. Their frustration causes a smile to cross the face of the mysterious figure hiding in the shadows by the fireplace.

Suddenly, from out of nowhere appears a tall, sandaled man in a long, white robe. You can almost feel His commanding presence. Even the figure in the corner seems to sense it as he slinks deeper into the darkness.

As the newcomer approaches the table, two individuals step aside to make room for Him. For a moment He just stands there, studying each piece of the fractured image. As His eyes shift from fragment to fragment, Laurie thinks she sees a tear course down His cheek.

Then she finds herself watching something strange. The sandaled man is stretching forth the fingers of His right hand. Slowly, yet purposefully, He is touching the corner of the photograph. Now He's sweeping His hand across the whole thing.

Laurie blinks. Then she blinks again. Miraculously, the image is knitting itself together. Soon not a seam nor a sign of stress is visible. The photograph has been restored.

One observer gasps. Another sinks to his knees and starts to pray. Laurie, who by this time is projecting herself into the scene, feels compelled to speak.

"I don't know for sure who you are, kind Sir, or how to express my gratitude. Words seem so inadequate. But thank you. Thank you for restoring what was broken, for making it whole once again."

Laurie pauses, then continues. "I don't want to rob this moment of any of its sacredness, but I do want you to feel at home. Here, please take a seat. I'd like to get to know you."

"I'd like that too," the stranger answers in a voice that rings with familiarity.

Laurie starts, then shouts with recognition, "It's You! The Lone Voice belongs to You! It is You who keeps persisting when we are too busy to listen. It is You who corrects us when we are wrong. And it is You who cares enough to focus us when we are fractured.

"Oh, God, forgive me. I almost didn't listen. I almost missed the joy of getting to know You. Please don't ever let me get so fractured again that I give up life's most important relationship. Draw me close, so close I can feel each beat of Your heart. Comfort me. Nudge me. Channel me. And keep me. For I love You, Lord. You're my Savior, my Deliverer, and I want You to be the Controller of my life.

With these words, Laurie reaches out to grasp the Stranger's hand, but contact eludes her. The Man in the white robe has vanished. With His departure, her dream ends.

She sits up in bed, wide awake. But she is strangely at peace. As she looks toward the window, she can see the promise of an emerging dawn. Carefully so as not to awaken her sleeping husband, she tucks the blanket under his chin.

Then she slips out of bed, grabs her robe and her Bible, and heads for the den. As her bare feet plod along the carpeted hallway, she can feel her heart surging with anticipation. It's the beginning of a brand new day. The whole world is waiting. And this time she is ready.

 Appendix A

We Are Free!

1. To say no to good opportunities in order to say yes to the best
2. To choose to do a few things without feeling we have to do everything
3. To render our services creatively without comparing ourselves to others
4. To prioritize the people in our lives, giving some more attention than others
5. To make the sacrifices God requires and stop making those He doesn't
6. To concentrate on relationships instead of activities
7. To refuse to feel guilty when we are not
8. To read the Bible for a heart message, instead of out of obligation
9. To pray on the run, knowing we're "practicing the presence of God"
10. To know we're important to God even when we're not doing anything
11. To filter what we're hearing, even from the church, through the Word of God
12. To "seek first the kingdom of God and His righteousness," knowing other things will then fall into place.

How to Extend Yourself Without Getting Overextended

1. Control your involvement or it will control you. When it does, you may lose your marriage, your family, even your fellowship with God. Is it worth it?

2. When opportunities for service arise, choose the best from the good. Chances are, *all* opportunities that tempt you will be good ones. That's where self-restraint comes in.

3. Realize you can't meet the needs of everybody. Only God can do that. In fact, the needs of some people are so great that if we spent every moment of the rest of our lives trying to meet them, we would still come up short. And there would be no time to reach out to those whose needs we *could* meet. So let's beware of "spiritual leeches," people who wittingly or unwittingly drain our very blood and do it in the name of Christian obligation.

4. Eliminate in order to concentrate. Choose to do "one thing" (see Phil. 3:10), and focus on doing it with all your heart. This "selection of ministry" will require cancelling, refusing, and restructuring. But the benefits will be eternal.

5. Realize the effectiveness of your ministry will be in direct proportion to the amount of God's Word you assimilate. Notice this is not necessarily the amount of time you spend in the Word of God. Long devotional time can well have minimal effects if the truths we are learning are not applied. It's making God's Word part of us that counts.

6. Minister from your overflow, never from your reserves. It helps to think of ourselves as containers with only so much to give. We pour a little here, a little there, and before we know it, the pitcher is upside down and we're banging on the bottom. Is there a drop left in there? Fill to overflowing and let ministry come from the spillover. That way we lose nothing. And everybody gains.

7. Take time to withdraw and refresh yourself. Schedule time away. Laugh at something funny. Listen to a music tape. Create an instant "sanctuary." It's not the activity that counts; it's the time "apart."

8. *Keep eternity's values in view.* It would be tragic to come to the end of our lives and learn we had lived in vain. Keeping the Lord first will eliminate this fear. The apostle Paul said, "For me to live is Christ." Therefore he could say at the end of his life, "I have fought a good fight, I have finished the race, I have kept the faith. Now there is in store for me the crown of righteousness." (2 Tim. 4:7). What a close to a life lived for God's glory!

Peg's Plan for Personal Preservation

1. Praise: I will begin each day with a God-exalting Scripture verse: 1 Chronicles 29:10–13:

> *Praise be to You, O Lord*
> *God of our father Israel*
> *from everlasting to everlasting.*
> *Yours, O Lord, is the greatness and the power*
> *and the glory and the majesty and the splendor,*
> *for everything in heaven and earth is Yours.*
> *Yours, O Lord, is the kingdom;*
> *You are exalted as head over all.*
> *Wealth and honor come from You;*
> *You are the ruler of all things.*
> *In Your hands are strength and power*
> *to exalt and give strength to all.*
> *Now, our God, we give You thanks,*
> *and praise Your glorious name.*

I will recite this passage before my feet hit the floor. It will be my defense against a negative attitude all day. (Se Ps. 34:1.)

2. Present: I will present my body a living sacrifice to God, part after God-created part: "Here's my mind (mouth, heart, etc.), Lord. Use it today in a way that pleases You." (See Rom. 12:1.)

3. Plan: There is nothing that gives me a greater sense of accomplishment than crossing items off a list. So I'll enumerate what I want to accomplish today, but I'll keep my list flexible enough for God to rearrange it. (See Isa. 32:8.)

4. Purpose: I will remind myself several times today why I was created. Then I will ask, "Am I glorifying God right now?" I will remember it's possible to do church work and *not* do it for God's glory just as it is possible to do secular work and *do* it for God's glory. I will not compartmentalize my activities. (See 1 Cor. 10:31.)

5. Plug in: I will remember God's power source is as close as my Bible, but I must connect in order to benefit from it. So I'll read it, meditate on it, memorize it, sing it, listen to it—whatever—until it becomes part of me. (See Isa. 55:11.)

6. *Pray:* I'll "practice the presence of God" today, listening for His voice in the cacophony of sounds around me. When I hear God speak, I will respond. I'll also set aside time to do nothing but pray. (See 1 Thess. 5:17.)

7. *Pour out:* I'll look for opportunities to share God's truth today. Whenever I'm tempted to think I don't have anything to give, I'll remember that as a child of God I have *everything* to give, but I must keep my supply filled to overflowing. (See 2 Kings 4:3–6.)

8. *Play:* I'll set aside time for just me. I'll sleep, exercise, groom, snack, read, play, relax, and laugh. I'll seek to maintain this "temple" in which God dwells, remembering, though, a more lasting temple is reserved in heaven for me. "Thank You, Lord, for both the temporary and the permanent. I want to respect both." (See Prov. 17:22.)

Endnotes

1. Hannah Whitall Smith in *The Christian's Secret of a Happy Life*, quoted in "Reflections," *Christianity Today* (13 September 1993), 50.
2. Annie Chapman with Maureen Rank, *Smart Women Keep It Simple* (Minneapolis, Minn.:, Bethany House, 1992), 15.
3. Mother Teresa, *Words to Love By* (Notre Dame, Ind.: Ave Marie Press, 1983), 79.
4. Dr. Martin Luther King, Jr., quoted in "Points to Ponder," *Reader's Digest* (April 1992), 181.
5. Tim Hansel, *When I Relax I Feel Guilty* (Elgin, Ill:., David C. Cook Publishing Co., 1979), 63.
6. Elizabeth Cody Newenhuyse, *The Woman with Two Heads* (Dallas, Tex.: Word Publishing, 1991), 173.
7. Tim Stafford, *Secrets of the Christian Life* (Carol Stream, Ill.: Zondervan, Campus Life Publications, 1979), 50.
8. Tim Hansel, *You Gotta Keep Dancin'* (Elgin, Ill.., David C. Cook Publishing Co., 1953).
9. Brother Lawrence, *Practicing the Presence of God* (Old Tappan, N.J.: Fleming H. Revell Co., 1953).
10. Peg Rankin, *Yet Will I Trust Him* (Ventura, Calif.: Regal Books, 1980), 123.